The Feng Shui Dictionary

The Feng Shui Dictionary

Lillian Too

HarperCollins*Publishers*
77–85 Fulham Palace Road,
Hammersmith, London W6 8JB
www.harpercollins.co.uk

First published by HarperCollinsPublishers 2009

The material in this book was originally published as
Feng Shui Fundamentals: Eight Easy Lessons in 1997 and
The Illustrated Encyclopedia of Feng Shui in 1999.

1 3 5 7 9 10 8 6 4 2

© Lillian Too 2009

Lillian Too asserts the moral right to be
identified as the author of this work

A catalogue record of this book is
available from the British Library

ISBN 978-0-00-784900-0

Printed and bound in China by
Leo Paper Products Ltd.

All rights reserved. No part of this publication may be
reproduced, stored in a retrieval system, or transmitted,
in any form or by any means, electronic, mechanical,
photocopying, recording or otherwise, without the prior
written permission of the publishers.

Contents

What Is Feng Shui?	vii
A through Z entries	1
The Harmony of Yin and Yang Energies	12
Compass Feng Shui	55
The Five Elements	97
Rooms That Are Too Yin or Too Yang	130
The Luo Pan Compass	164
The Eight-sided Pa Kua Symbol	192
How to Deflect Poison Arrows	206
Feng Shui Tips for Interiors	224
The Chinese Calendar	285

What is Feng Shui?

Feng Shui means "wind and water." In the literal sense it refers to the topography of the earth, its mountains, valleys, and waterways, whose shapes and sizes, orientation, and levels are created by the continuous interaction of these two powerful forces of nature.

To people of Chinese origin all over the world, Feng Shui connotes a mystical practice that blends ancient wisdom with cultural superstitions. This broad body of traditional knowledge lays down guidelines for differentiating between auspicious and inauspicious land sites. It also provides instructions on how to orient homes and design room layouts to enhance the quality of life dramatically.

In the family home, well-oriented Feng Shui features work to create harmonious relationships between husband and wife and between children and parents, foster good health, and attract abundance and prosperity. They bring good fortune to the breadwinner, build good reputations, and strengthen descendants' luck – children who will bring honor and happiness to the family in the future.

In business premises, good Feng Shui creates opportunities for growth, elevates prestige in the community, attracts customers, raises profits, and expands turnover. Employees stay loyal and a pervasive aura of goodwill ensures smooth working relationships.

Good Feng Shui results when the winds and the waters surrounding your home and work space are harmonious and well balanced. Bad Feng Shui, on the other hand, brings illness, disasters, accidents, burglaries, and financial loss. It results in lost opportunities, fading careers, squandered wealth, and collapsed reputations. Above all, bad Feng Shui causes grave unhappiness, and it can sometimes even provoke tragic consequences for the reputation and well-being of the family unit as a whole.

Feng Shui is an exciting component of ancient Chinese wisdom – a science that goes back at least 4,000 years to the days of the emperors and mythical legends. That it has so brilliantly survived the centuries bears testimony to its potency. In recent years there has been an extensive revival of interest in its practice, particularly in the West, where the study of Feng Shui began as a New Age phenomenon, but has now attracted mainstream attention.

The current popularity of Feng Shui stems from the widespread appeal of its simple logic. While its many theories and guidelines are based on the Chinese view of the universe, the fundamentals are easily understood and widely applicable. Its laws and tenets relate to simple basic concepts that advocate living harmoniously with the environment, creating balance in the living space, and blending in with the natural landscapes of the world: the contours of the land, the terrain of the earth, the rivers and waterways of the world, sunlight and moonlight, vegetation, orientations, and directions – in short the winds and waters of the living earth that surrounds us.

Note

Words in bold have their own entries in the dictionary which the reader can refer to for further explanation.

Feng Shui ...

... advocates living in harmony with the earth's environment and energy lines so that there is balance with the forces of nature.

... contends that the environment is crowded with powerful, but invisible energy lines.

... says that some of these energy lines are auspicious, bringing great good fortune, while some are pernicious and hostile, bringing death and the destruction of happiness.

... offers ways of arranging the home so that these energy lines become harmonious and bring prosperity and harmony, rather than loss and discord.

... instructs us in the clever harnessing of auspicious energy lines – generally referred to as **Sheng Chi**, the dragon's cosmic breath – making sure they meander gently through the home and accumulate and settle, thereby bringing good fortune.

... teaches us to avoid, deflect and dissolve inauspicious energy lines – also know as **Shar Chi** – which represent the **killing breath** caused by secret **poison arrows** in the surroundings.

... strenuously warns against sleeping, working, sitting, eating, and generally living in places that are hit by these pernicious hostile energy lines.

Almanac

The Chinese book of auspicious dates. The Tong Shu (also T'ung Shu), or the Chinese Almanac, is one of the oldest books in the world. It originated more than 4,000 years ago and contains the largest number of divination systems ever gathered together in a single volume. The heart of the book is its calendar, which is based on the Chinese **Ganzhi**, or lunar system, of calculating the days and seasons of the year. The Tong Shu contains auspicious dates for undertaking a variety of daily activities, from selecting the best days for starting a new business to washing and cutting one's hair, to performing harvesting and planting rituals. The Chinese Almanac is one of the most comprehensive and traditional collections of Chinese beliefs and practices in existence. The Tong Shu contains references to Feng Shui practice that are based on **flying star** calculations of auspicious and inauspicious days for undertaking a variety of domestic and business activities.

Altar

Let your altar face the door directly. There are basic rules for propitious placing of altars. The Chinese generally believe it is extremely auspicious to have the altar directly facing the front door, so that the minute we walk into our homes we can see the altar. From a Feng Shui point of view, it is also recommended that the altar be placed in the northwest section of the house or living room, since this sector represents the **Chien trigram**, which in turn symbolizes heaven and heavenly deities. Irrespective of where you place your altar, you should always ensure that your **Buddha**, Kwan Yin, or any other deity is in an elevated position. The Feng Shui dimension most suitable for altars is at least 60 inches (150 cm) high. The altar must always be clean. Keeping lights on continuously, apart from representing auspicious light offerings to the deity, also attracts good **Chi** energy.

Amulets

A practice popular with the Chinese is the wearing of amulets that are believed to ward off bad luck caused by wandering spirits in the environment. The Chinese believe that young children are particularly vulnerable to these wandering spirits, and many parents obtain special symbols from the temple or use those specially created for them by Taoist priests. It is debatable if this practice can be considered as part of Feng Shui practice. The author herself used to wear protective amulets as a child.

Antidotes

Feng Shui antidotes, or cures, are available for almost all Feng Shui problems. Some work better than others and correctly choosing which antidote to use is one of the skills of the Feng Shui master. There are many different antidotes and these are generally summarized as follows. Use:

- bright lights to dissolve bad energy.
- **Yang energy** – lights, sound, and bright colors – to overcome excessive **Yin energy**.
- windchimes, especially four-rod windchimes, to diffuse bad energy.
- the **Pa Kua mirror** to deflect killing energy.
- bells and singing bowls to purify stagnant space.
- crystals to soften excessive **Yang energy**.
- colors to correct element imbalance.
- curtains and blinds to deflect bad energy.
- the compass to change to more auspicious directions.
- element therapy (*see* "The Five Elements," pp. 97–9) to correct disharmony.

Antiques

Danger of harmful left-over energy. The danger with displaying antiques in the home is that you are unlikely to know the luck of the people who last owned the piece, or the quality of the **Chi** that still clings to the antique. It may contain very negative energy that could bring bad luck to whoever possesses it. It is particularly risky to keep antique cannons and firearms in the house, because these, especially if they come from clan homes, are likely to have "tasted" blood before.

Aquarium

A water feature that brings good Feng Shui. It is a good idea to activate the wealth sector of the office (the southeast corner) by introducing a water feature. An aquarium containing lively fish symbolizes growth and activity. You can also activate the southeast corner of your home with an aquarium. However, do not place your aquarium or fishpond on the right-hand side of your front door (standing on the inside looking out) for this may cause husbands to stray or encourage a roving eye.

Archways

Can be auspicious if they are not overdone. The curved shape of the arch is an auspicious shape because there are no angles to send out harmful **poison arrows** to the surrounding living space. An archway is more conducive to harmonious Feng Shui than square doorways in the home. Archways also suggest the circular shape that represents the element of gold. They are especially lucky when placed in the northwest and west of the home. They should preferably not be seen in the east and southeast.

A

Armchair

Formation in **Landscape Feng Shui**. A vivid way of describing the perfect location for your home is the "armchair formation" of **Landscape Feng Shui**. This symbolism is part of the **Form School**. The armchair formation suggests that ideally the home should have higher land at the back (known as the **black turtle**) to provide support, like the back of an armchair. The left-hand side of the home should be higher, because this is deemed to be the place of the **green dragon**. The land to the right of your home is the place of the **white tiger** and should be lower than the dragon. If land on your right is higher than land on your left, the tiger becomes overbearing and dangerous. In front of the home is the **crimson phoenix**, which acts as the "footstool." Ideally there should be a small hump just in front of your home.

Arrowana

With its silver scales and sleek, swordlike body, the arrowana has long been used by Chinese businessmen in Malaysia, Singapore, and Thailand to bring good fortune. Also known as the "dragon fish," it is best kept singly or in threes or fives, but never in pairs. When the arrowana is well fed and healthy, it emits a pink or golden glow; it is this glow which is said to bring good fortune. If you wish to keep arrowanas, you should make sure they are well fed and well-looked after. Only strong, vibrant arrowanas have the capacity to bring you great wealth. The aquarium which houses this fish should not be cluttered with water plants or seaweed or have too much sand. A large, bare aquarium will serve to accentuate the beauty and the abundance of the fish. The aquarium is best kept in the north corner since this is the water corner. The aquarium can also be kept in the east or southeast, which are wood corners. This is because water is harmonious with wood. Never keep arrowana in your bedroom.

Arrows

Symbolic of killing energy. Among the most dreaded Feng Shui taboos are secret **poison arrows** caused by hostile structures in the landscape.

Art

There are Feng Shui implications in the art you hang in your home or office and these can cause good or bad Feng Shui without you being aware of it. Indeed, the subject, color, and orientation of paintings all have Feng Shui implications; it is therefore important to consider your paintings seriously when you hang them. The rules for hanging paintings are:

- Avoid hanging abstract art in colors that clash with the element of the wall on which you are hanging the painting. Thus, do not hang art depicting metal objects or those that are painted substantially in white or metallic colors in the wood corners (the east or southeast). In the destructive cycle metal destroys wood; the **elements** are in disharmony and the painting is creating problems for the wood corner. If you occupy a room in this corner you will suffer from the clash of energies.
- If you wish to hang portraits of the monarch, or perhaps the founder of your company, the best wall would be the northwest, since this activates the luck of the **Chien trigram**. This **trigram** represents the patriarch, or leader, and hanging a painting of a leader in the northwest creates exceptionally good **mentor luck**.
- The best art to have in the office is landscape art, because Feng Shui is about the landscape. If you can fold landscape into your office in an unobtrusive manner, you will enjoy harmonious Feng Shui. A mountain painting behind your

seat symbolizes support. This is one of the best features to create for good Feng Shui in the office.
- A painting of water or a stream in front of your desk at work effectively simulates water bringing great good fortune to your office. Paintings of rivers, lakes, and waterfalls are therefore to be hung in front of you and never behind.
- Similarly, a painting or a picture of a big, open field in front of you symbolizes the **bright hall**. This symbolism is enormously lucky, whether real or as a painting, since it suggests a complete and total absence of obstacles. A big, open field suggests that everything will be smooth in your business and in your career.
- Make use of the good fortune symbols of Feng Shui by hanging paintings of fruit and flowers that symbolize abundance and auspicious fortunes.
- Avoid paintings of wild animals such as lions, tigers, leopards, and eagles inside the home or office. They serve you excellently outside, to protect you and your family, but inside the home they can turn against you and bring ill-fortune, illness, and bad luck.
- Avoid so-called character or intellectual art that shows wizened old men or art that records the tragedies of our age. It is far more auspicious to hang paintings of new life and happy occasions. Remember that everything hung on the walls of your home or office affects the Feng Shui of your home or office.

The Harmony of Yin and Yang Energies

At its most basic, Feng Shui is a question of balance, but this balance is related to the complementarity of opposites, expressed in terms of the Yin and the Yang. According to the Chinese, all things in the universe are either the female Yin or the male Yang, the dark Yin or the bright Yang.

Yin and Yang together make up the wholeness of the universe, which includes heaven and earth. Yin and Yang breathe meaning into each other, for without one, the other cannot exist. Thus, without the Yin of darkness, there cannot be the light of Yang; without the cold temperature of Yin, there cannot possibly be the warmth of Yang, and vice versa.

When there is balance between Yin and Yang, the wholeness of the universe is represented. There is good balance and prosperity, health, well-being, and happiness. Feng Shui practice always includes a Yin–Yang analysis of room space, land configurations, sunlight and shade, dampness and dryness, bright and pale colors, and solids and fluids. Rooms that are too Yin are not auspicious; there are insufficient life energies to bring prosperity. Rooms that are too Yang are said to be damaging because there is too much energy, causing accidents and huge losses. Only rooms – and homes – with balanced Yin and Yang can be auspicious, and will be made even more auspicious if there is a good balance of Yin and Yang outside.

See "Rooms That Are Too Yin" and "Rooms That Are Too Yang", pp. 130–2.

Astrology

Chinese astrology, or fortune-telling, is often confused with the practice of Feng Shui. This is due to the overlap of basic concepts, such as those of Yin and Yang, and the theory of the five **elements** used in both sciences. Also, many practitioners of the art of divination, especially in Hong Kong, incorporate Feng Shui advice in their recommendations, notably those who use the Four Pillars method of divination.

This method is also known as the Paht Chee, or Eight Characters, and is based on the element that is discerned to be "missing" from one's astrological chart. The fortune-teller will advise siting a main door or a sleeping direction that energizes the element that is missing. This method thus uses the Five-Element theory exclusively and is also based on the subjective judgment of the person undertaking the astrological reading.

A second method of Chinese astrology is the Purple Star, said to be especially accurate in predicting good and bad periods of one's life. It is the nearest thing to Western astrology but the "stars" it uses in the chart are imaginary stars. Unlike Western astrology, Chinese astrology does not chart the movements of the planets.

Auspicious Feng Shui

This means enjoying various types of Feng Shui luck. Good fortune in Feng Shui usually refers to eight categories of luck and these include:

- enjoying wealth, success, and prosperity;
- having good family life and relationships;
- enjoying good health and having a long life;
- enjoying a good love life/marriage;
- having good descendants' luck, i.e. children who bring honor to the family;
- enjoying power and the patronage of mentors;
- having a good education; and
- enjoying a good reputation and becoming famous.

Specific Feng Shui measures can be energized to encourage each of these eight different types of good fortune. All the different schools of Feng Shui stress these eight types of human aspirations, and if even one of these aspects of good luck is missing, life, and therefore the Feng Shui, is deemed to be incomplete.

Bad Feng Shui

The antithesis of good luck. Misfortunes caused by Feng Shui often occur frequently and come so thick and fast that you will not fail to see a pattern developing. Thus, if everyone in the home takes turns getting sick, encountering loss, accidents, and problems at work, you should consider if some structure or alignment may be hurting your home. Almost every kind of negative Feng Shui feature can be diffused to some extent. Certain configurations and arrangements may be harder to deal with than others but all negative arrangements can be ameliorated.

Balance

Means applying the Yin and Yang concept to Feng Shui. Feng Shui is about balance. This balance is struck between two cosmic forces, Yin and Yang. These two opposing yet complementary energies shape the universe and everything in it. Together, they form a balanced whole known as the Tao – or "the Way" – the eternal principle of heaven and earth in complete harmony. Achieving good Feng Shui has much to do with balancing the concepts of Yin and Yang. One should never forget, when practicing the science of Feng Shui, that balance is everything. Without balance, your Feng Shui will not be auspicious. *See* "The Harmony of Yin and Yang Energies," pp. 12–13, **Yin Energy**, **Yang Energy**.

Balconies

Must be oriented correctly vis-à-vis the entrance. It is not a good feature to have balconies that open in a straight line from the front entrance of the home. This creates an inauspicious flow of energy.

Bamboo

An excellent Feng Shui plant signifying longevity. It is also an extremely useful Feng Shui tool. Bamboo stems can be used in the same way as windchimes, with hollow rods or wooden flutes, to counter the heavy **killing breath** of an overhead beam. They should be hung in pairs, slanted toward each other at the top, in such a way as to allow the auspicious **Chi** to rise up to counter the **killing breath** being emitted from the overhead beam. Because bamboo stems emit no tinkling sound to provide the necessary **Yang energy**, to transform the **Chi** into friendly and auspicious energy the bamboo stems should be tied together with a piece of red string. The color red will bring out the **Yang energy** needed.

    Bamboo stems are also an excellent tool for slowing down **Chi**. If you have long corridors in your house, the rooms at the end of such corridors suffer from **Shar Chi**, the **killing breath**, rushing headlong toward them. This fast-moving **Chi** can be slowed down using bamboo stems hung in the same way as described above, with a red piece of thread tied between them. These hollow stems encourage the poisonous **Chi** to rise up through them and in the process turn the Chi into friendly **Sheng Chi**. The best way to counter a long corridor is to block the room it hits by using a screen or divider of some sort; bamboo stems, flutes, and windchimes can only do so much to help. If these Feng Shui antidotes are, however, much smaller than the corridor itself the best solution is to use both stationary and hanging dividers.

Banking

The business of banking belongs to the water element, and thus the most effective Feng Shui enhancer for a bank is water. Building auspicious water features in the north or the southeast is especially recommended.

Barbecues

Because barbecues represent fire (as do all cooking appliances, stoves, ovens, and so forth), they are best held in the south of the garden, which is ruled by the fire element. This activates the corner that brings recognition and **fame luck** to the family. It is also the sector of the middle daughter, so holding barbecues here will assist her in her grades and her personal development. If you are not able to locate the barbecue in the south corner of your garden, you should at least ensure it is not placed in the east or southeast, as these sectors are wood sectors. The fire from the barbecue will (symbolically) burn the wood, thus burning away your **wealth luck** (southeast) and **health luck** (east).

Basement Apartments

These are usually not auspicious. Feng Shui does not recommend living below road level. Basement apartments are therefore not the best units to live in. If you have no choice you can enhance the **Chi** by installing bright lights at the entrance. This should "raise" the energy, encouraging **Chi** to flow into the apartment. If the basement apartment opens into a garden at the back, the Feng Shui will be considerably improved.

Bathrooms

Bathrooms are similar to toilets in the way that Feng Shui views them. They are not good to have in the house from a Feng Shui viewpoint. Try to minimize the size and décor of your bathrooms and keep the doors to your bathrooms closed at all times. Bathrooms should never be too large.

Beaded Curtains

A Feng Shui cure for afflicted doorways. The placement of doors within the home has great Feng Shui significance. You should never have two doors directly facing each other across a corridor. This confrontational positioning will bring about quarrels and misunderstandings between the members of the household, and particularly between the two people whose doors face each other. To soften the negative effect of such a layout, short of changing the placement of the doors completely, hang a beaded curtain across the doorway. This way, the door always appears to be closed. However, if one door faces part of another this has a worse effect. In such a situation, it is advisable to try to place something between the doors, such as a plant, which can act as a divider. Beaded curtains in this instance will not be a suitable solution.

Beams

Protruding overhead beams cause Feng Shui problems inside the home and office. You can either hang a five-rod windchime or hang two hollow bamboo stems tied with red thread to overcome the negative **Chi**. Do not sit directly underneath exposed overhead beams, especially structural beams.

Bedrooms

Important rooms that should always enjoy good Feng Shui. The main thing to remember is that the bedroom is a place of relaxation and rest. The energies that prevail in the bedroom should thus be more Yin than Yang, since a bedroom that is too Yang will cause the occupant to be too active, which may cause difficulties in sleeping. Because of this, many Feng Shui masters warn against activating the bedroom with too many good fortune symbols. Such symbols, which may work well in the other parts of the house, may work against you in the bedroom.

Water features are generally auspicious but they do more harm than good in the bedroom. Sleeping with water behind you will cause you to be robbed or to suffer a financial loss. Note that water does not only mean aquariums, fountains, and fish bowls. Paintings of water should also be kept out of the bedroom. It is, however, acceptable to decorate your bedroom in blue, a color of relaxation and calm. Black represents water and this color should not be a prominent feature of your bedroom.

The inclusion of mirrors is one of the most common mistakes in modern bedroom interior design. Mirrors are frequently used to create a sense of space. Whether the mirrors are attached to cupboards in the bedroom, or on the ceiling, the reflective edges of mirrors send out **Shar Chi** onto the sleeping couple. This will cause quarrels and misunderstandings, as well as ill-health. Mirrors also bring a third party into the marriage when they reflect the sleeping couple, causing husbands and/or wives to be unfaithful. Note that anything with a reflective surface, even television sets, which resemble a mirror, should be kept out of the bedroom. If you have mirrors that you cannot take down, cover them with a curtain. Similarly, television sets should be covered with a cloth each night before you go to sleep.

Open shelves should be covered up anywhere in the house, not just in the bedroom, where they do most harm. If you have such shelves facing your bed while you sleep each of the shelves will be sending little **poison arrows** toward you throughout the night. It will only be a matter of time before you fall ill. If you cannot close the open shelves with doors, another solution is to ensure the shelves are lined with books whose spines are set flush with the edge of the shelf, thus getting rid of the shelves.

Flowers and plants, especially growing plants, are potent symbols of **Yang energy**, and are not suitable for the bedroom. If you place plants in a girl's bedroom, this will work against her in the romance stakes. If plants feature in the bedroom of a couple they will quarrel frequently. The only time flowers and plants are justified in the bedroom is when someone is recuperating from an illness and needs **Yang energy** to recover.

Your sleeping direction is a most important consideration if you are to benefit from good Feng Shui. It is therefore vital that your head is pointed in one of your four good directions while sleeping. Check your good and bad directions using the formula based on your **Kua number** (*see* "Compass Feng Shui," pp. 55–8.)

Beds

Sleep in a bed with Feng Shui dimensions. A Feng Shui bed has auspicious dimensions and is decorated with colors that harmonize either with the element of the corner in which the bed is placed, or the element of the year in which you were born. To be safe, it is better to use the element of the corner; this allows the bed to be auspicious for more than one person (i.e. for you and your partner or spouse). Beds with headboards are better as they provide support. Because a bedroom is a place of rest, too much **Yang energy** is bad and can cause sleepless nights. If you wish to use red, a dark red or maroon is better than a bright, chilly red. Bedspreads are also better in plain colors. Avoid any abstract designs with arrows and triangles: these represent the fire element, which is very bad for the bedroom. It also symbolizes many **poison arrows** attacking you while you sleep.

Bells

Use tinkling bells to improve turnover in your business. Chinese shopkeepers have long been aware of the efficacy of tinkling bells in attracting customers into their stores. When hung on the door or on a door handle, the ringing of these metal bells creates good **Chi** each time someone enters the store. This brings in the luck required to make people purchase your products, enhancing your store's turnover. This method is particularly effective for stores selling personal items such as jewelry, clothes, and accessories.

    The bells can be made of any type of metal. They should be tied with a red ribbon to increase their effectiveness, as this activates their intrinsic **Yang energy**. The ideal number of bells is six or seven, although most shopkeepers only keep one set of bells. Tiny bells can also be placed inside the store anywhere along the west or northwest wall or high up on the ceiling directly facing the door. This will entice the precious **Sheng Chi** to enter the store. The bells need not be seen, as long as they work. Their function is a symbolic one and as long as they tinkle a little each time the door is opened they will bring increased luck for the store. In the old days, bells were usually used to announce good news, being symbols of good fortune.

Birdbaths

Excellent water features suitable for the north, east, and southeast of your garden. Ensure that the water is clean at all times, replacing the water daily if necessary. The more birds you have visiting your birdbath, the better the energy that is created by this water feature.

Birds

Represent the auspicious phoenix, especially when they are placed in the south part of your home. Thus, keeping sculptures of any kinds of birds in your south-facing garden, or on the south side of your living room, brings luck in the form of opportunity. Live birds in captivity, however, spell bad Feng Shui, captivity being symbolic of retarded growth, and this may well curtail chances of progressing in one's career.

Birth Dates

These are required in calculating Eight Mansions and Four Pillars Feng Shui. Birth dates are required in the calculation of personalized lucky and unlucky directions. There are two main schools of Feng Shui requiring the date of birth. The first is the Eight Mansions formula, which works out your **Kua number**. With this number you will be able to refer to a table that details your four auspicious and four inauspicious directions. The second is the Feng Shui method using your Four Pillars. This is the same as the Eight Characters (Paht Chee) method of fortune-telling. This method requires not just the date but also the hour of your birth. In using your birth dates, however, always remember that in using any of the Chinese divinitive sciences you must know your date of birth according to the **lunar calendar**.

B

Black Turtles

Celestial creatures that bring great good fortune. The black turtle is believed to be one of **four celestial creatures** that bring good fortune as well as good health and protection. The arrangement of the numbers on the **Lo Shu magic square**, one of the most important symbols of analysis in **Formula Feng Shui**, is said to have originated from the back of a black turtle which swam up from the shores of the Lo River. The arrangement of the numbers one to nine within the square is supposedly based on the markings found on this ancient turtle. Whichever way you add up the numbers, whether diagonally or in a straight line, the numbers always added up to nine. The black turtle is one of the four animals that make up the auspicious "armchair" formation in **Landscape Feng Shui** (or the **Form School** method of Feng Shui). The armchair is made up of the **green dragon** on the left, the **white tiger** on the right, the black turtle at the back (for support), and the **crimson phoenix** in front (as a footstool). When a home is built in the middle of these four animals, precious **Chi** is attracted and created there, leading to much good luck for the occupants of the home.

The black turtle is a popular symbol of good fortune for the home. Displayed either as paintings, or figurines, or kept as a pet tortoise or terrapin, the symbolic Feng Shui created is extremely auspicious. These smaller cousins of the turtle are believed to bring the same good fortune as the turtle. If you wish to keep a terrapin or tortoise, keep it in the north sector of the house, but keep only one, since this is the number of the north. Do not worry that your pet will feel lonely without a mate: terrapins are natural loners.

Blue Flowers

Good for the north, east, and southeast parts of the garden. Colors are powerful Feng Shui enhancers and playing with colors is a creative way of perfecting the Feng Shui of your garden. Blue flowers symbolize the element of water, thus planting them in the north, southeast, and/or east parts of the garden will activate the luck of these corners. The north sector is for **career luck**, the southeast is for **wealth luck**, and the east is for good health.

Blue Roofs

One of the danger signs in Feng Shui. Try to avoid having a blue roof since this signifies water on the top of your house. Change the tiles if you have to.

Boardrooms

These can be energized to bring excellent corporate Feng Shui. The best location for the boardroom of a corporation is the place that is diagonal to the entrance, deep inside the office. Boardrooms should not be on the top floor.

Bonsai

Though beautiful, bonsai trees are artificially stunted and do not give good Feng Shui. They are particularly harmful to businesses and commercial enterprises since they are the direct opposite of what needs to be energized for growth. If you have a passion for bonsai trees and simply must have them somewhere in your home, avoid placing them in the wood corners (east and southeast) of your house or garden. Placed in the north, they cause the least harm.

Book of Changes, or *I Ching*

The major source book of Feng Shui, and probably the main source book of most of China's cultural practices. The seasoned wisdom of thousands of years has gone into the makings of the I Ching. Both branches of Chinese philosophy – Confucianism and Taoism – have their common roots in this ancient classic, known also as the Book of Changes. The I Ching alone, among all the Confucian Classics, escaped the great burning of the books under Emperor Chin Shih Huang Ti in 213 B.C.E. The origins of the I Ching go back to mythical antiquity, as a book of divination and as a book of wisdom. All that is great and significant in Chinese cultural history takes inspiration from the I Ching – aspects of the many related principles and symbols of the Chinese predictive sciences, its view of the trinity, heaven, earth, and man, the concepts of Yin and Yang, balance and harmony, positive and negative forces, good fortune and misfortune, are all derived from interpretations of the texts and judgments of the I Ching's 64 hexagrams.

Bookshelves

These represent knives cutting into you and are bad Feng Shui. If you have exposed bookshelves in your office or study, change them into cupboards by covering them with doors. Unless you do this, the shelves will act as deadly **poison arrows**, causing you loss and illness.

Boulders

Signify earth energy and are an excellent Feng Shui remedy. Tied with red string, a boulder is an effective antidote if placed in a bathroom that is in the wrong place in your home.

Boundaries

For Feng Shui analysis, boundaries must be accurately measured and taken. Feng Shui is best approached as a method or technique. When using the compass methods it is vital to get measurements and compass readings correct. This enables you to establish the parameters of your space more accurately. Feng Shui works when the space has been accurately demarcated according to directions, locations, and **elements**.

Breath of the Dragon

The cosmic **Chi**.

Brick Walls

Feng Shui remedy for blocking out unwanted and inauspicious sights, especially structures that are sending **killing breath** to the home.

Bridges

Bridges near your home will be auspicious if they have three, five, or nine bends. They may be straight or curved, beamed, arched, suspended, or floating. They can be pavilion or corridor bridges and can be made of stone or wood, including cane. In China, bridges that are intended to enhance the Feng Shui of gardens are usually built of stone, and the arch formed is usually in the shape of a semicircle.

Bright Hall

An excellent Feng Shui situation. One of the most auspicious Feng Shui features a building can have is for the main door to open out onto a park, a football field, or any kind of empty land. This creates what Feng Shui masters describe as the **bright hall** effect, where auspicious **Chi** can first collect before entering the home. You should not try to achieve the **bright hall** effect at all costs. If, say, there is a statue or structure that forms a poison arrow directly facing the front door, it is better to give up trying to create the **bright hall** effect and the auspicious good fortune that it is supposed to bring than to suffer from the deadly **Shar Chi** from the poison arrow. Remember always to practice defensive Feng Shui first.

Brooms

Brooms, mops, and cleaning materials should never be left around the home. Keep them hidden away. As well as sweeping away bad luck, they can also sweep away good luck. Brooms are particularly bad fortune if left in the dining room, as they symbolize your rice bowl and livelihood being swept away. Brooms have another use in Feng Shui. They can be an effective tool to ward off burglars and intruders from the house when placed upside down against the wall and facing the front door, but outside the home rather than in. Leave a broom outside only at night; put it away during the day.

Buddha Statues

Holy objects must have good Feng Shui. Paintings and statues of Buddhas should be regarded as holy objects. Do not place them below, facing, or near bathrooms. The best place for displaying your antique Buddha statue is the northwest of your entrance hall or living room.

See also **Altar**.

Buildings

In modern Feng Shui, these simulate mountains. In old days, **Form School** Feng Shui examined surrounding hills and mountains to determine the quality of the Feng Shui terrain. Today, the practice of Feng Shui has shifted to big cities, where buildings form the landscape and surroundings for homes and offices. Because Feng Shui is symbolic, buildings are now analyzed in the way that surrounding hills used to be.

Bulbs

Usually considered to be good fortune flowers; they represent hidden gold. These are regarded as lucky flowers and indeed symbolize the blossoming of hidden talents and abilities when they bloom. The Chinese are fond of growing bulbs around the lunar New Year, especially the narcissus, because of their association with the advent of spring.

Business Feng Shui

This focuses on creating wealth and prosperity luck. In the West business Feng Shui is becoming increasingly important as more career professionals and entrepreneurs recognize the potency and effectiveness of Feng Shui in enhancing turnover and improving bottom lines. Retail businesses can benefit enormously from simple Feng Shui enhancers.

Cactus

Cacti and any other types of prickly plants create tiny slivers of poisonous energy which can cause bad luck, illness, and misfortune. They should not be placed in the home and are better outside, where they take on a protective role. Their thorns then counter any **Shar Chi** heading in your direction. Inside, rather than counter **Shar Chi**, they create harmful **killing breath**.

Cannon

To be used as a last resort to counter big **poison arrows**. Cannons are very effective in deflecting **killing breath** and pointed, hostile objects aimed at your front door. The negative force sent out can be very potent. Antique cannons that have been to war are the most powerful of all.

Career Luck

Can be energized with Feng Shui. Good career luck manifests itself in increased opportunities. It does not suggest instant success. When using Feng Shui to activate luck at work be prepared for an increasing workload and responsibilities as well as more opportunities for advancement. Activate the north part of your home, office, or personal space. Since the north is of the water element, a good way to energize this corner is to place an aquarium of energetic fish there, such as guppies. Their vigorous swimming will create the precious **Yang energy** needed to give your career a boost. Advanced practitioners can use the Feng Shui formula to activate professional **career luck**. It is also a good idea to make yourself an auspicious work desk whose dimensions have been measured with a Feng Shui ruler.

Cash Register

In retail businesses registers can be energized with coins and bamboo. Increase sales by taping three old Chinese coins tied with red thread, Yang side up, onto the side of your cash register. The Yang side has four Chinese words, the Yin side has two. Important files can also be treated in the same way to enhance Feng Shui at work. Alternatively, hang hollow bamboo stems above the cash register, also tied with red thread. The bamboo ensures that you will stay in business for a long time. Let the stems hang perpendicular with their tops tilted slightly toward each other.

Ceilings

Should neither be too low, nor have hostile designs. A ceiling lower than 8 feet (2.5m) suggests you will be weighed down with problems; it should clear the tallest person in the house by at least 4 feet (1.2m). Avoid corner angles or threatening, ornate designs. Beams should be avoided unless they are an integral part of the entire ceiling and especially if they stand alone. Paint your ceiling white or in a bright color, and never black or blue, both of which are very inauspicious.

Chandeliers

Create excellent Feng Shui if placed just inside or outside the home. They encourage good **Chi** to enter the house and they work just as well inside or outside the home. They are especially good when placed in the southwest, where the combination of fire (lights) and earth (crystal) brings wonderful romance and love luck to the members of the household. Try to activate the southwest of the whole house with a chandelier, rather than the southwest of a single room. The effect will be more powerful and will benefit the entire family.

Chen Trigram

This **trigram** symbolizes the dragon, thus a strong Yang line pushes upward below two broken Yin lines, which give way. Chen represents Spring, thunder, growth, and the eldest son, and is placed east on the **Pa Kua**.

Chi

The dragon's cosmic breath and the key to good Feng Shui, it brings good fortune. The concept of Chi is central to the understanding and practice of Feng Shui. Chi is the word used to describe an intrinsic force or energy that is invisible to the eye but can nevertheless be felt and is very potent.

Chi Kung

A form of martial training that allows you to "feel your Chi," its slow exercise movements are believed to enable practitioners effectively to move **Chi** energy within them. Such exercise is believed to help overcome serious illnesses.

Chien Trigram

The ultimate Yang **trigram** that signifies the patriarch. The first **trigram** in the **I Ching**. Made up of three unbroken lines, Chien is placed in the northwest quadrant of the **Yang Pa Kua**. Since this **trigram** symbolizes the patriarch the northwest is said to be the corner of any home that governs the luck of the male paternal.

Childlessness

Can sometimes be helped using Feng Shui. If you are having problems conceiving, suggest the man changes his sleeping location or direction. Use his **Nien Yen** direction, which will be based upon his personal **Kua number**.

Children

The manifestations of good descendants' luck. Children represent the next generation and this is one of the eight aspirations addressed by Feng Shui practice. The west side of the house is the place to energize for ensuring descendants' luck but the children of the house, especially the sons, should sleep in the east part of the house in rooms located in their personal auspicious locations, based on **Compass Feng Shui**.

Clothes

Affect the type of energies you attract. Clothes have a bearing on your luck. Wearing torn clothes is very inauspicious. It attracts poverty energy, which often translates into the most severe kind of ill-fortune. Wearing unflattering clothes has the same effect; as well as making you feel bad about yourself, it depletes your **Yang energy** and causes you to feel lethargic.

Coins

One of the more potent of symbolic Feng Shui tools. They represent wealth and are superb for activating Feng Shui for wealth. Authentic old Chinese coins can be used as Feng Shui coins. The square hole in the middle has Feng Shui meaning. The circle and square together represent heaven and earth. Three coins should be tied together with red string and hung on the inside of your front door to symbolize the money already inside your house. *See also* **Cash Register**.

Color

Amplifies the **elements**. Good color combinations bring good luck. Color therapy in Feng Shui is directly related to the concept of the five **elements**, each of which stands for a certain color or colors. These are summarized as:

Wood	browns and greens
Fire	reds, yellows, and orange
Metal	white, gold, silver, bronze, and chrome
Earth	ocher and light yellow
Water	blues, purple, and black

Each color on its own is neither good nor bad. Combinations of colors cause good and bad luck and this is again based on the destructive and productive cycles of the **elements**.

Some special combinations that are excellent luck: vermilion with gold; dark rich purple with chrome or silver; black and white.

Good color combinations: two blues one green; two browns one red; two reds one yellow; two yellows one white; two whites one blue.

Unlucky color combinations: two blues one red; two reds one white; two whites one green; two greens one yellow; two yellows one blue.

Columns

In the home square, freestanding columns can cause severe Feng Shui problems. Their sharp edges can send out poisonous **killing breath**, which should be deflected and dissolved by placing plants against the edges. Alternatively, wrap mirrors around the columns. Columns should never be facing the main front door, either inside or outside, where they represent bad Feng Shui. In such a case, the door or the column should be moved.

Compass Feng Shui

This technique uses compass directions to create auspicious Feng Shui using formulas based on the **Pa Kua**, **Kua numbers** and the **Lo Shu Magic Square**. *See* "Compass Feng Shui", pp. 55–8.

Compass Feng Shui

Compass Feng Shui offers very precise use of formulas that spell out specific ways of investigating auspicious or inauspicious directions for orienting doors and entrances, the placement of furniture, and the direction for sleeping.

There are formulas to calculate individual auspicious and inauspicious directions based on personal **Kua numbers**, and others for working out lucky and unlucky sectors of buildings from month to month and from year to year. The formulas address both the space and time dimensions of Feng Shui. They differentiate between east and west groups of people and buildings, offering methods for balancing personal energies with those of the environment. There are also formulas that address specific types of luck, particularly **wealth luck**, that have to do with the correct placement of water and its direction of flow around the living area.

Compass formula Feng Shui is a little more complex to learn than **Form School** Feng Shui. However, it is less subjective, which makes it easier to practice. One of the formulas used in Compass Feng Shui is given here:

The Kua Numbers Formula

There is a powerfully potent method for discovering personalized auspicious and inauspicious directions based on birth dates. Calculate your **Kua number** as follows:

Check against the Chinese calendar (*see* pp. 285–93) to make sure you use your Chinese year of birth.

MALES
- Take your year of birth.
- Add the last two digits.
- If the result is more than 10, add the two digits to reduce them to a single number.
- Subtract from 10.
- The answer is your Kua number.

Example:
Year of birth 1936
$3 + 6 = 9$
$10 - 9 = 1$
The Kua number is 1.

FEMALES
- Take your year of birth.
- Add the last two digits.
- If the result is more than 10, add the two digits to reduce them to a single number.
- Add 5.
- The answer is your Kua number.

Example:
Year of birth 1945
$4 + 5 = 9$
$9 + 5 = 14$
$1 + 4 = 5.$
The Kua number is 5.

The **Kua numbers** are the key to unlocking your auspicious and inauspicious directions. **Kua numbers** one, three, four, and nine have east, southeast, north, and south as the auspicious directions. The specific ranking of each of these directions and the precise type of luck they activate for you make up the more detailed aspects of this formula and differ for each of the **Kua numbers**. It is sufficient to know that with these **Kua numbers** you are an east group person. The inauspicious directions for you are, therefore, the other four, the west group directions.

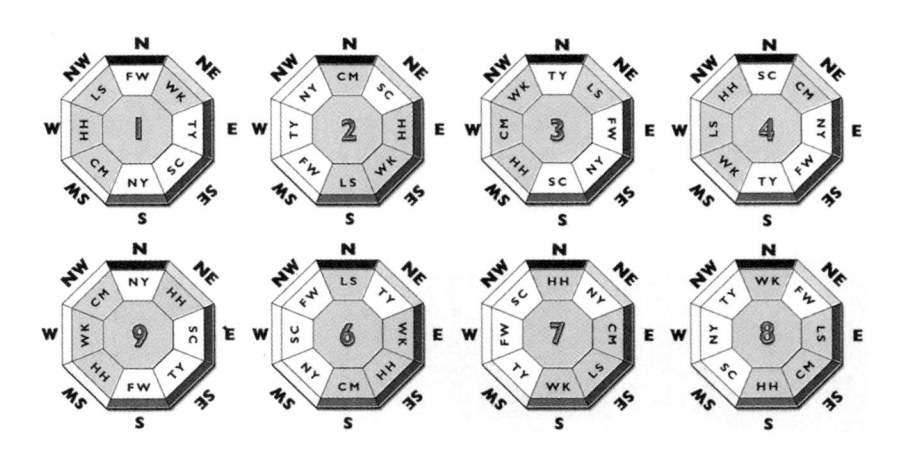

Kua numbers two, six, seven and eight have west, southwest, northwest, and northeast as the auspicious directions. Again the specific ranking of each of these directions differs for each of the **Kua numbers**, but these are west group directions. The inauspicious directions for you are thus the other four, east group directions.

There is no **Kua number** 5 in this system. Males who have a **Kua number** of 5 should use the number 2 and females who have a **Kua number** of 5 should use the number 8.

Computers

Computers do not cause bad Feng Shui. When placed in the west or northwest they can become energizers in these corners. Use screensavers that bring good fortune. Display images according to the corner where your computer is standing.

Conceiving

As well as using the husband's **Nien Yen** direction, also hang a painting of children near the marital bed. Alternatively, place a small representation of the dragon next to the bed to simulate the precious **Yang energy** needed.

See also **Childlessness**.

Cooking

Cooking has serious Feng Shui connotations. Feng Shui warns against placing stoves in the northwest of the kitchen. If possible, try to avoid having the kitchen itself in the northwest corner of the house. The northwest corner represents the patriarch, or primary breadwinner of the family; placing the stove or kitchen there is like burning the luck of the patriarch. The northwest is also the corner that represents heaven, the stove in the northwest suggests "fire at heaven's gate," and this is most inauspicious. The northwest is also of the metal element and a stove represents fire, the only element capable of destroying metal.

Corners

Protruding or missing corners can cause problems. Protruding corners inside the home create vertical sharp edges that send out negative energy, thereby creating havoc in households. Nullify this by placing a tall bushy plant against the corner. The second type of protruding corner appears in a room that juts out of a regular-shaped house. Such additions to the layout of the home make it lucky or unlucky, depending on where the main door is located. This applies to the Feng Shui of the entire house and therefore affects anyone living in it.

Location of main door	Lucky location of addition	Unlucky location of addition
North	West and northwest	Southwest and northeast
South	East and southeast	North
East	North	West and northwest
West	Southwest and northeast	South
Southeast	North	West and northwest
Northeast	South	East and southeast
Southwest	South	East and southeast
Northwest	Southwest and northeast	South

Missing corners can be lucky or unlucky for the home in question also depending on the location of the main front door. If the missing corner is unlucky you can try to solve the problem by adding a mirror wall to one side of the missing corner, but only if the mirror is not directly facing anything harmful. If it is, shine a bright light into the corner or if possible build an extension. If the missing corner is not hurting the luck of the house you do not need to do anything.

Location of main door	Lucky missing corner, corner, requiring no cure	Harmful missing corner, requiring a cure
North	Southwest and northeast	West and northwest
South	North	East and southeast
East	West and northwest	North
West	South	Southwest and northeast
Southeast	West and northwest	North
Northeast	East and southeast	South
Southwest	East and southeast	South
Northwest	South	Southwest and northeast

To investigate the effect of missing corners on the luck of specific individuals, apply the formulas that investigate an individual's lucky and unlucky directions, either the Eight Mansions or **Pa-Kua Lo-Shu** formula that uses your **Kua number** to determine the effect of the directions on your luck, or the Four Pillars method.

Corporate Logos

See **Logos**.

Corridors

Long, straight corridors become **poison arrows**. They symbolize arrows sending **Shar Chi** throughout the office or home and cause disharmony in human relationships. If your room is badly placed on a corridor, break the flight of a poison arrow by placing plants and windchimes along it, to reduce the negative impact of the arrow.

Cosmic Breath

See **Chi**.

Cranes

Birds that are one of the most popular symbols of longevity among the Chinese. They are often seen in Chinese art or are drawn in with Sau, the **God of Longevity**. Sculptures or other symbolic representations of cranes should be placed in the south or west of your garden.

Crimson Phoenix

The celestial creature of the south. The "king of all the feathered creatures of the Universe," the phoenix is said to appear once every thousand years when times are auspicious and a good leader sits on the throne. Phoenixes are said to signify wonderful opportunities for bringing a good name, wealth, and prosperity to the family. Placed in the south the phoenix is represented in Feng Shui by low foothills.

Cross

Directly opposite your house or office, a cross brings bad luck. Crosses are inauspicious signs, whether they appear as church spires or as structural features, because they send **Shar Chi** toward your house. If you can use a door that does not face a cross as your main door, do so, if not, hang a **Pa Kua mirror**.

Crystals

Excellent Feng Shui energizers, especially when they are placed in the southwest corner. Natural quartz crystal clusters are among the best symbols of mother earth and are extremely effective when used to energize the southwest corner (the big earth corner). The southwest also governs the luck of romance, love, and family happiness. This is applicable irrespective of your particular **Kua number**. If you energize the southwest corner of your living room, everyone living in the house will benefit. Before displaying the crystal, it should be soaked for seven days and seven nights in salt (sea) water to dispose of any negative energies it may be carrying.

Curtains

Effective Feng Shui tools, curtains have a dual function in Feng Shui: they can block out excessive sunlight or views of harmful structures in the environment. In Feng Shui what cannot be seen is deemed to have "disappeared." Curtains can be used to enhance the Feng Shui of your living space, whether it be home or the office. Study the colors best suited to each corner of the room according to the compass direction. This comes from the corresponding **elements** of the directions. For instance, hang a dark blue curtain in the north, the east, or the southeast. Blue is synonymous with water, which is good for these three directions – the north because it belongs to the element of water, the east and southeast because these wood corners will benefit from the water element of the curtain. In the same way, red, yellow, and pink curtains will be excellent in the south, southwest, and northeast; green will be good in the east, southeast, and south; white and metallic colors (gold or silver) are auspicious in the west, northwest, and north; browns will be good in the east and southeast; purples and lilacs will be good in the north, east, and southeast.

Cycles of Chi

The enhancing, controlling, and weakening cycles. This relates to the five **elements** and Feng Shui practice requires an appreciation of the interactive cycles of the five **elements** to understand the cycles of **Chi**. There are three important cycles to incorporate into Feng Shui analysis. The enhancing or producing cycle explains how one element can help another (or type of **Chi**) to exhibit its quality and ability. Some masters prefer to describe water as "enhancing" wood. When a tree is watered, it grows. When a fire is fed with wood it burns. In the weakening cycle, wood helps fire to burn and in the process weakens or diminishes itself. Thus within the productive cycle is the seed of weakening energy for one element. The controlling or destroying cycle (some masters prefer the former term) explains how one element can control and suppress another. It does not necessarily destroy the other element since energy, or **Chi**, cannot really be destroyed. One element can dominate in a particular circumstance over another. Thus a metal knife cuts a piece of wood to transform it. It is controlling the shape of that piece of wood.

Design Motifs, Shapes, and Colors

All these have Feng Shui connotations. In Feng Shui, Art Nouveau is to be preferred to Art Deco simply because the former suggests something more rounded and curved than the latter. However, in the design of motifs and decorations for interior decoration, it is useful to develop different motifs for each of the five **elements** and then to use them according to the directions symbolized by each element. For example, use the water motif for rooms in the north (water corner) part of the home since such rooms will benefit from having the element there enhanced. Use this table to determine the element motifs most suitable.

Location of rooms	Element motifs/symbols
North, east, and southeast	Water motifs and symbols
South, southwest, and northeast	Fire motifs and symbols
West and northwest	Metal motifs
Southwest and northeast	Earth motifs
East and southeast	Wood motifs

Desks

Can be energized to attract excellent work luck. The desk is an excellent object for Feng Shui energizing. Energize your desk top with objects that symbolize the five **elements**. Do this by demarcating on your desk top a **Lo Shu** grid and then, using a compass, mark out the corresponding compass direction of each of the grids. Energize your desk according to the **Lo Shu** grid direction in the table. Place the following:

East	A bowl of fresh flowers
Southeast	A small green plant
West	Your telephone
Northwest	Your computer terminal
North	Your cup of coffee
South	A light or something red
Southwest	A lapis globe
Northeast	A crystal paperweight

In addition, check your **Kua number** and find out your best sitting direction. With the aid of a compass, mark out the direction that you should be facing to bring you good luck. Sit like that as much as possible. Finally, make sure that you have a clear view from your desk, unencumbered by office paraphernalia.

Destructive Cycles

These refer to the negative cycle of the five **elements**. The theory of **Wuxing**, or the five **elements**, is a central axis of Feng Shui practice. According to the theory all things in the universe can be categorized as one of the five **elements** – wood, fire, earth, water, and metal. There is a productive and destructive cycle to these **elements**.

Dining Room

In Feng Shui, a most important room. Here, food on the family table can be symbolically doubled with mirrors facing the table. The dining room also benefits the family if it is located in the middle of the home since this signifies the family's presence at the heart of the home.

The dining room should always be higher than, or on the same level as, the living room. If you live in a multistory house, make sure your family dines on the higher level. If you have more than one dining room in your house, make sure the one most regularly used is on a higher level. The dining room should not be next to the bedroom; this creates a lot of unsettling **Chi** in both rooms. It is also very inauspicious to have a toilet too close to the dining room; if you have this, keep the door closed at all times.

Do not let the dining room be located at the end of a long corridor; it is extremely inauspicious for the family to eat in such an unlucky room. To energize the "stomach" of the home further, hang paintings of luscious flowers and ripe, juicy fruits.

Dining Table

There are four auspicious shapes for dining tables – round, square, rectangular, and the eight-sided **Pa Kua** shape. Of these, Chinese families prefer the round shape because this symbolizes the smooth procession of everything. The round shape also signifies gold, which means money. Thus round tables are said to symbolize the creation of wealth and prosperity.

Door

These are especially important in Feng Shui analysis. The size and number of doors as well as the way they are placed in relation to each other in the home have Feng Shui implications. The orientation of the main door is especially important; ensure that it is not being hurt by hostile structures in the outside environment.

Double Happiness

This activates good marriage luck. Displaying the double happiness symbol — the Chinese word for happiness written twice — is excellent and popular Feng Shui.

It also activates the wedding luck of people of marriageable age. If you are hoping to find romance or a partner, try placing the double happiness symbol in the southwest corner of your house or a large boulder in the southwest corner of your garden. This incorporates both element and symbolic Feng Shui.

Doubling

The concept of doubling wealth is part of Feng Shui amplification. Doubling anything makes the outcome more auspicious. Thus a wall mirror should double the food on the dining table. This signifies wealth and is auspicious. The daily income of a restaurant or store should be doubled with a wall mirror that reflects the cash register.

Dragon

The most important symbol both in Feng Shui and in Chinese folklore. The celestial dragon is the ultimate symbol of good fortune in every Chinese divinitive science and is central to the practice of Feng Shui. The direction traditionally associated with the dragon is the east; thus, placing an image of a dragon in the east side of the office or home will bring much good fortune. Gardens can also be activated using the dragon symbol by simulating a dragon on the east side of the house with plants set in a winding flowerbed.

However, when using the dragon symbol, there are several taboos which must be noted: never place a dragon inside the bedroom – it is too Yang a symbol in a place of rest; dragons made out of wood, ceramic, or crystal are fine, but avoid dragons made out of gold, cloisonné, or other metals, since the metal element destroys the wood element (the element of the east); sitting at a desk bearing dragon imagery can bring much good luck, but not all people have sufficient **Yang energy** to sit at such a desk. *See also* **Chi**.

Drains

These can be made effective in creating wealth under the **Water Dragon** formula. The humble monsoon drain can be harnessed to bring extreme good fortune by applying the **Water Dragon** formula. The general guidelines about drains are that they should always be kept free flowing; blocked drains signify that all your ventures will meet up with obstacles. Drains should also be cleaned regularly and be flowing past your main door in the correct direction. The rule of thumb for the direction of water flow depends on the orientation of the main front door. This is summarized as follows:

- For homes where the main door faces north, south, east, or west, i.e. the cardinal directions (taking the direction from inside the house looking out), drains should flow past the main front door from left to right for the flow to be auspicious.
- For homes where the main door faces the secondary directions, i.e. southeast, southwest, northeast, and northwest, the drain should flow from right to left for it to be auspicious.

Driveways

The Feng Shui of driveways depends on how they approach the home. Long straight driveways that point directly at the main front door in the form of an arrow bring bad Feng Shui. To nullify the bad effect, allow the driveway to curve or meander. A circular driveway is most auspicious since the round shape signifies gold.

Early Heaven Arrangement

Refers to the arrangements of the **eight trigrams** around what is known as a **Yin Pa Kua**. This sequence of **trigrams** is placed on protective **Pa Kuas** used for deflecting the poisonous breath of harmful sharp structures in the environment. *See also* "The Eight-sided Pa Kua Symbol," pp. 192–3.

Earth

The element that most represents Feng Shui at work. Feng Shui is the luck of the earth, and the earth element is an important component in the correct practice of Feng Shui. At the same time the ultimate Yin **trigram**, which indicates the essence of the matriarchal energy so important in a home, is **Kun**, whose element is earth. The center of the home is also said to belong to the earth element. As such it is important that earth **Chi** should be present in healthy doses for a home to be lucky.

Probably the most effective symbol of the earth is the globe. When placed in northeast it assists in harnessing luck for the children. In the southwest and center of the home it magnifies and improves the luck of the family; in the west and northwest it often leads to prosperity. *See also* "The Five Elements," pp. 97–9.

East

The place of the dragon and of the wood element. The east signifies the essence of growth energy. The wood element is significant because anything requiring upward thrusting energy will benefit from being in the east. In the old days this was the place reserved for the heirs of the dynasties. Similarly, Feng Shui also advises that sons of the family will benefit from living in rooms that are located in the east. Since the east is of the wood element it also benefits from a presence of lush green plants and any kind of water feature. Always keep a healthy store of **Yang energy** in the east and do not allow stagnant energy to collect and accumulate because it is especially harmful.

East Group

This is part of the Eight Mansions **Pa Kua Lo Shu** formula. Based on **Compass Feng Shui**, you belong to the east group if your **Kua number** is 1,3,4, or 9 and the auspicious directions of people in the east group are north, south, east, and southeast.

East House

This is defined according to the direction of the main door. An east house is a house that has a main door facing west and northwest. This is part of the Eight Mansions formula of orientation. This particular guideline can create problems of implementation for those who want to arrange the orientation of a main door that needs to face west or northwest but who have to live in a west house.

Education Luck

A simple way of energizing the luck of education is to activate the earth element of the northeast corner of the bedroom. Place a globe or a cluster of natural crystals to strengthen the earth element of this corner.

Eight Precious Objects

Eight treasures believed to be extremely auspicious. Placed together or singly the eight treasures are considered to be extremely auspicious and precious by followers of Buddhism. To attract good fortune to occupants, practitioners of Symbolic Feng Shui usually display the treasures as embroidered fabric screens hung on doors leading into bedrooms and other important rooms. They also portray them as symbols on porcelain or similar pieces of art. Each symbol may also be tied with red thread and worn separately as a lucky charm.

- *The double fish symbol* is believed to ward off evil intentions and is often worn as an amulet. Place it near the entrance of the home to keep away anyone with bad feelings for you.
- *The lotus* brings every kind of good fortune. Grown at home it has the potency to turn bad luck into good luck.
- *The conch shell* (or any kind of seashell) attracts auspicious travel luck. Place it in your living room. Seashells picked up from the seashore should be cleaned and soaked in salt water for at least a month before being used.
- *The dharma wheel* (or wheel of law) represents the power of the heavenly energy; a painting or representation of this wheel is said to lead to positive spiritual development.

- ***The precious vase*** (or urn) placed near the entrance of houses attracts **Chi** and encourages it to settle and accumulate. Keep vases empty if placed outside the house but keep them full when inside the house. Fill these vases to the brim with seven varieties of semiprecious stones. If you wish you can transform them into **wealth vases** and put a small amount of earth taken from a rich man's home.
- ***The parasol or umbrella*** (or canopy) is an excellent symbol of protection. It is believed to ward off burglars when placed near the front part of the home or in the lobby.
- ***The mystic knot*** signifies the neverending cycle of good luck turning into bad luck and into good luck again. Buddhists also see it as the neverending cycle of birth and rebirths. In Feng Shui it is a popular symbol of neverending affection and devotion.
- ***The banner of victory*** symbolizes success in all your endeavors. It is often depicted as a long victory flag similar to those used by ancient Chinese armies. The banner of victory is a particularly auspicious symbol to display if you are in politics, the army, or working in government. It brings an elevation in rank.

Eight Trigrams

These are the principal symbols of Feng Shui analysis. Placed around the eight sides of the **Pa Kua**, the eight **trigrams** are three lined combinations of broken and unbroken lines. The unbroken lines are said to be Yang lines while the broken lines are said to be Yin lines. The eight **trigrams** are **Chien**, **Kun**, **Kan**, **Li**, **Ken**, **Chen**, **Tui**, and **Sun** and they make up the root of the 64 hexagrams that in turn make up the **I Ching**. Understanding the essence and deep significance of these **trigrams**, as well as the way they are placed around the **Pa Kua**, unlocks the secrets of the eight-sided **Pa Kua** symbol.

Elements (Wuxing)

The theory of the five elements. The elements are water, wood, fire, metal, and earth and their interactions make up the theory of **Wuxing**, which is central to the practice of Feng Shui and to the understanding of Chinese forms of divination and fortune-telling. *See also* "The Five Elements," pp. 97–9.

Elephant

The symbol of fertility, and good for the luck of sons, the elephant is also the symbol of strength, sagacity, and prudence and is one of the four animals representing power and energy, the other three being the tiger, the leopard, and the lion. The elephant is also one of the seven precious treasures of Buddhism and in Thailand it is regarded as a most precious creature. The Chinese believe that the elephant creates auspicious descendants' **Chi**. If it is placed inside the home childless couples can be blessed with children; those wishing for sons to carry on the family name are advised to lodge a stone on the back of a precious elephant and display it prominently in the bedroom so as to ensure the birth of a male child.

Elevated Structures

These should be examined to see their effect on doors. If such structures as tall buildings or overpasses are placed too close to your main door they are said to cause serious Feng Shui afflictions to both the door and the house. Block off such structures with trees.

Empty Spaces

See **Bright Hall**.

Energy

Likened to the dragon's breath, or **Chi**. Energy is probably the most accurate translation for the word **Chi**. Another is breath, as in the dragon's cosmic breath. Energy offers the essence of what **Chi** can do, both positively and negatively.

Enhancers

Good fortune symbols that, if correctly placed, create good Feng Shui. There are many different symbols of good fortune that can be used to enhance the Feng Shui of corners and rooms. Most Feng Shui techniques also make use of element methodology to enhance the different corners to energize different categories of good fortune.

Entrances

These are exceedingly important in Feng Shui, referring to the main entrance into the house, not to the gate. Entrances are where the auspicious **Chi** enters. If entrances suffer from Feng Shui afflictions the **Chi** that enters is said to be similarly afflicted. There are also Feng Shui formulas based on sex and dates of birth that offer advice on the kind of orientation that brings the best kinds of luck. If you live in an apartment the entrance into the apartment building is as important as the door into your own apartment. At least one should be oriented in a direction that is auspicious for you. If you live in a house with a garden and you have more than one door into the house, the main door is defined as the one that is most frequently used.

Exterior Feng Shui

Exterior Feng Shui, i.e. the Feng Shui of your surroundings, must not harm your home. Thus garden Feng Shui becomes a significant and important part of Feng Shui practice because the landscape and environment around your home define its Feng Shui. If the exterior Feng Shui is harmful, then anything you do inside the home becomes afflicted. Good Feng Shui therefore begins from the outside.

Fame Luck

This can be energized by improving the Feng Shui of the south, which governs the luck of recognition and respect. To energize this luck install bright lights in the south side of the home. If your entrance faces south, certain schools of Feng Shui also suggest this will help you get a good name.

Family Feng Shui

If you wish to enhance the harmony of relationships within the family, the center of the home should be energized. Do this by placing the television room or the dining room in the center of the home, then place a bright light to enhance and magnify the earth mother.

Family Portraits

An effective method of creating family closeness is to hang a family portrait in the living or family room. Every member of the family should be included and, to symbolize happiness, each person should be smiling. Arrange the family in a way that creates a shape most suited to the father, or patriarch, of the family.

- *A triangular arrangement* is particularly effective when the father is born in a fire or earth year. Make sure that he is at the apex of the triangle. This arrangement creates the element of fire, signifying precious **Yang energy**.
- *A wavy arrangement* is effective if the father is born in a water or wood year. This arrangement creates the water element. It is a Yin shape and is excellent when there is excessive **Yang energy** in the house, i.e. when there are many sons and no daughters. The father should be in the center and, so as to create the wavy shape that symbolizes water, the heads of others in the picture should be at different levels.

- *A rectangular arrangement* suggests the wood element, and is the most common. The heads of everyone in the picture are on the same level. This arrangement also suggests a balanced and regular shape and is suitable if the father was born in a wood or fire year.
- *A square arrangement* is similar to the rectangle and is suitable for small families. This shape suggests the earth element and is suitable for everyone, since the earth element also signifies the family. It is especially good if the father was born in a metal year, since earth produces metal in the cycle of **elements**.

Family Room

A family room in the center of the house creates harmony. The house will be balanced; the heart of the home is the room in which the family spends time together.

Fire

One of the five **elements**, symbolized by the direction south. Fire is placed south in the **Later Heaven Pa Kua** because it is the location of the **Li trigram**, which stands for fire. To energize the luck of opportunities and the luck of recognition, install a bright light in the south. This not only magnifies fire energy but also brings in the Yang essence so vital for success luck. *See also* "The Five Elements," pp. 97–9.

The Five Elements

A core concept of Feng Shui practice is the theory of the five elements and their productive and destructive cycles. All Chinese astrological sciences, acupuncture, physical exercises such as **Chi Kung**, and medicine depend on an understanding of the theory for diagnoses and cures. In Feng Shui, understanding the nature and cycles of the elements vividly enhances the potency of its practice. This is because the Chinese view all things in the universe as belonging to one of the element groups. As each compass direction has it own ruling element, every corner of every home or room is also deemed to belong to one of these elements. The five elements are wood, fire, water, metal and earth.

Feng Shui practice takes account of element relationships by ensuring that the elements of objects, direction, and locations in any room do not destroy each other. Element relationships, based on their productive and destructive cycles, must, therefore, always be taken into account when any Feng Shui diagnosis or cure is being considered.

The Elements

- *Wood* is represented by all shades of green. Its season is spring. Big wood lies in the east, while small wood is in the southeast. Symbols of the wood element are plants, paper, furniture, and all things made of wood. In numerology, wood is represented by the numbers three and four. The Chinese horoscope lists the tiger and the rabbit as wood animals.
- *Water* is blue or black. Its season is winter and its direction is north. This is a Yin element and its number is one. Objects that represent water include aquariums and fountains. Animals belonging to this element are the rat and the boar.
- *Fire* is red, considered a very auspicious Yang color. Its season is summer and its direction is south. Symbols of this element are bright lights. Its number is nine. Fire animals are the snake and the horse.
- *Metal* is signified by the metallic colors, gold or silver, and also white. Its season is fall and its directions are west (small metal) and northwest (big metal). Objects of the element are windchimes, bells, coins, and jewelry. Its numbers are six and seven. The metal animals of the Chinese horoscope are the rooster and the monkey.

- *Earth* is represented by all shades of brown. It is the element of the center and it represents every third month of every season. Its directions are southwest (big earth) and northeast (small earth). Its numbers are two, five, and eight and its horoscope animals are the ox, the dragon, the sheep, and the dog.

Productive and Destructive Cycles

In the productive cycle of the elements, fire produces earth, which creates metal, which makes water, which produces wood, which makes fire.

In the destructive cycle of elements, wood devours earth, which destroys water, which extinguishes fire, which consumes metal, which demolishes wood.

Fish

Keeping fish is believed to bring good Feng Shui. Fish represent success. If you have an aquarium, it is best displayed near the front entrance or in the living room. The arrowana fish is a particularly auspicious fish to keep. If you cannot keep live fish, the symbol or image of a fish on a vase or in a painting will be good enough. Display these near your front door or living room. *See also* **Arrowana**.

Fishponds

These are excellent water features. Fishponds are auspicious not only because of the symbolic meaning of the fish derived from Chinese folk tales but because fish are especially effective when it comes to energizing corners as well. Fishponds are particularly beneficial in the north (water), southeast or east (wood), for they are the element of water and water is compatible with both water and wood (which it nurtures). Keeping fish also creates **Yang energy** which encourages **Chi** to circulate, bringing a place to life.

Flowerbeds

Rectangular or square flowerbeds are better than round ones. The combination of the wood element with the metal element is created when you have round flowerbeds. This is inauspicious. Better to combine wood with wood, i.e. grow your flowers and plants in rectangular flowerbeds. This among other features will determine the Feng Shui of your garden.

Flowers

Excellent Feng Shui energizers for love and for the benefit of daughters of the house. Fresh flowers are best but once they are past their prime they should be thrown out to prevent harmful **Yin energy** accumulating. Flowers with thorns are also not good Feng Shui; remove these from roses, for example, before displaying them. Flowers in the bedroom of a healthy person are also not advisable: these will bring too much **Yang energy** into what is meant to be a place of rest. For those who are sick, however, flowers in a bedroom (as in a hospital room) will give the sick person much needed **Yang energy**.

In Feng Shui fake flowers are as good as real. They are excellent energizers of fresh **Yang energy** and are especially effective in the living room. Dried flowers, however, are purveyors of **Yin energy** and are not recommended in the home. Also avoid preserved or pressed flowers.

Flying Star Feng Shui

Flying star Feng Shui is a potent compass formula. It deals with the time dimension of Feng Shui, where the significance of changing forces during the different periods is taken into account. This school of Feng Shui makes use of the intangible influence of numbers, together with the pattern of **Lo Shu** numbers as they move in a time cycle in the **lunar calendar**.

This formula can tell you the sectors of your home that are auspicious for a certain time period, while warning you against sectors which are inauspicious. You should spend most of your time in rooms that are "lucky" during the period in question, while trying as far as possible to keep the unlucky sectors quiet. For example, if you have an aquarium in the north (which is usually a good sector in which to place an aquarium), and that sector is particularly unlucky for the period in question, it is better to move the aquarium to another sector of the house or another corner of the room.

With flying star the prosperity and luck of any residence or commercial building can be investigated and determined. The ruling numbers in each period correspond to the numerical values for each of its ages. For example, in the Lower Period, the ruling numbers are 7, 8, and 9. These numbers come from the **Lo Shu** grid and their significance relates to the **trigrams**. They are also associated with the five **elements** with each having a specific name and distinct connotation. The term "flying star" derives from the stars flying from room to room.

Form School

A part of the landscape method that looks at shapes and contours in the landscape. Form School Feng Shui is another name for **Landscape Feng Shui**. This looks at the lie of the land, the shape, elevation, and appearance of structures, the flows of water, the contours of the land, and the terrain. Form School Feng Shui is often regarded as classic Feng Shui and it is, since it directly addresses the luck of orientations and the impact of the winds and waters.

Formula Feng Shui

A method that requires accuracy of application. Formula Feng Shui represents a range of different methods that make up **Compass Feng Shui**. Formula Feng Shui takes the subjectivity out of Feng Shui and it always works when the measurements of dimensions and readings of the compass directions are accurate.

Fountains

Fountains are popular features for energizing water but are more suitable for public places such as parks and shopping malls. They are not suitable for corporate head offices since the direction and flow of water downward can symbolize water flowing toward the building (which is excellent) or away from the building (which is bad).

Four Celestial Creatures

The **green dragon** (east), the **white tiger** (west), the **crimson phoenix** (south), and the **black turtle** (north). The four celestial creatures of Feng Shui each bring a specific aspect of luck to the house they collectively embrace. The dragon brings wealth and prosperity; the turtle brings patronage and support; the phoenix brings opportunity and recognition; the tiger brings protection against the dark forces. Together, and when oriented correctly vis-à-vis each other, the celestial creatures symbolize perfect Feng Shui.

Foyers

These should be brightly lit to attract good Feng Shui and to raise the **Chi**. If you do not have a foyer, try to ensure the door opens onto space and that the entrance is not cramped.

Frogs

The Chinese regard frogs and toads as creatures that bring auspicious luck. It is believed that a family of frogs living in your backyard can protect you from bad luck. The three-legged frog is particularly auspicious and is usually found with three gold coins in its mouth, signifying the bringing of gold into the house. Place the frog diagonally across the room from the front door, facing inward, not outward, which symbolizes gold going out. Keep frogs out of the kitchen, bathroom, and toilet to avoid bad **Chi** accumulating, and out of the bedroom.

Front Doors

An important focus of Feng Shui analysis. This refers to the main front door, the Feng Shui of which largely determines the Feng Shui of the entire home. It is thus vital to get the Feng Shui of the main door auspicious. *See also* **Doors**.

Fu Dogs

Important guard dogs that offer protective Feng Shui. Fu dogs (also known as the Chinese unicorn) are traditionally used by the Chinese to protect against bad luck. Chinese homes are rarely without them. Size is immaterial but they should be in proportion to the size of the house they are guarding. Place them high up on either side of the gate or at table level, and on a stand rather than directly on the floor.

Place your Fu dog according to the element of the location. If you are placing it on a gate and the corner where the gate is located is east, placing a pair of metal Fu dogs will be more effective. Gold controls the wood element of the east.

Fuk, Luk, Sau

The three star gods of health, wealth, and happiness. These are never worshiped, only displayed. They are enormously popular since they symbolize health, wealth, and prosperity, which actually means everything. Few Chinese homes are without these star gods. The best place for them is the dining room in a suitably elevated position.

Do not place them lower than the people in the room and do not place them in the bedroom. *See also* **Gods of Wealth**.

Furniture

This can be designed to incorporate important Feng Shui guidelines. Feng Shui inspired furniture can be particularly pleasing because it will have few, if any, negative forces. Such furniture should never have any nails driven into it: components should be designed to fit mortise and tenon. The beautiful antique Ming chairs, for instance, are highly prized because nails were never used in making them. Secondly, the chairs are always nicely curved, with no sharp edges or corners.

    Modern furniture can imitate the concept and essence of this sort of furniture. Sofas should have sizeable back support and armrests. Tables and cupboards should have rounded edges. Bookshelves should have doors to shut out the killing energy of shelves, which resemble blades sending **poison arrows** into rooms. Avoid metallic furniture, which emits disharmony, and furniture with sharp pointed edges or furniture that is triangular in shape.

Ganzhi (or Ghanxi) System

The system upon which Chinese astrology is based. It is packed with cyclic symbols that are associated with the Chinese zodiac animals and the **elements**. Ganzhi comprises twenty-two symbols grouped into two sets, ten belonging to the heavenly (or celestial) stems and twelve belonging to the earthly (or terrestrial) branches. The stems refer to the five **elements**, with a hard (Yang) or soft (Yin) heavenly aspect for each. The **elements** are earth, water, wood, fire, and metal. They have a productive as well as a destructive cycle. The branches refer to earthly forces and are represented by the twelve animals of the Chinese zodiac — the rat, ox, tiger, rabbit, dragon, snake, goat, horse, monkey, rooster, dog, and boar. The animals control the hour, day, month, and year and represent periods of each. One can be born on a tiger day, in a rat month, at a snake hour, and in an ox year. The combinations express the eight characters which are said to rule one's destiny.

Each of the twelve years are further categorized according to the five **elements** (12 x 5) to produce sixty-year cycles. These cycles repeat themselves. The Chinese believe that the interactions of the twelve earthly branches and the ten heavenly stems rule the entire destiny of man and form the basis of Chinese astrology. In fact, they believe that this interaction controls everything in the universe.

Through years of observation, the Chinese have worked out associations between environmental changes and the lunar, seasonal and solar periods in each of the sixty-year cycles. This is the basis of the Chinese **Almanac**, or Tong Shu, under which auspicious days for undertaking a variety of tasks are identified (e.g. for getting married, for starting a business, or for moving house).

Gates

The design and orientation of gates can be used to attract good **Chi** flows. Gates should ideally have two doors and open inward rather than outward. It is very auspicious to design a gate with the center higher than the sides: this symbolizes the attainment of one's goals. If the center is lower than the sides, it signifies misfortune in your career. Note that your front gate is not your main door; thus, when choosing auspicious directions for your home, you should place greater emphasis on the main door to the house than on the gate leading into the property.

Gazebos

If correctly built, these can strengthen the **Chi** of the main door. Gazebos are considered as additions to the garden. Depending on the location of a gazebo, it can enhance or detract from the Feng Shui of the house, especially in relation to its position with the main door and whether it strengthens or weakens its **Chi**. *See also* **Greenhouses**.

Location of main door	Good for gazebo/greenhouse	Bad for gazebo/greenhouse
East or southeast	North	West or northwest
West or northwest	Southwest or northeast	South
North	West or northwest	Southwest or northeast
South	East or southeast	North
Southwest or northeast	South	Southeast or east

Globe

A potent representation of the earth element. Especially when made of a semiprecious material like lapis lazuli, quartz, or jasper, a globe is an excellent energizer for **education luck** when displayed in the northeast corner of a young college student's room.

God of Longevity

Sau Seng Kong, the ultimate symbol of longevity. The God of Longevity is an excellent symbol to place in any home and few Chinese do without him: he brings good health and long life. He is always shown carrying a peach and accompanied by the crane and the deer, all of which are also symbols of longevity. He is usually carrying a staff on which hangs the gourd that contains the nectar of the gods. Sau Seng Kong is also recognizable by his deep forehead and domed head, symbolizing his great wisdom. He may be displayed in a painting or as decorations on Chinese ceramics and art objects.

Gods of Wealth

Special deities placed in the home to generate **wealth luck**. The Chinese have several deities they regard as the wealth god. One of the most popular is Tsai Shen Yeh, who is often shown sitting on a tiger, to symbolize his control over this animal. In the lunar years of the tiger, displaying the God of Wealth is particularly auspicious. It is not necessary to pray to this deity; simply invite him into your home as a symbolic gesture. One can also hang a knotted cluster of nine Chinese coins tied with red thread, to activate the prosperity attributes of the coins.

    The best place to display the God of Wealth is on a table between 30 and 33 inches (76 and 84cm) high directly facing the door. Thus, the first thing you see upon entering your home is the wealth god, symbolically greeting the **Chi** coming into the home, transforming it into healthy prosperous energy that then flows through the rest of the house. If this spot is already occupied by the family altar, place the wealth god diagonally opposite the front door, facing toward it. Do not place your wealth god in the dining room or bedroom. Kwan Kung, usually regarded as a bringer of wealth, is another popular Chinese deity.

Goldfish

If you keep goldfish (they are lucky), place nine of them in an aquarium or goldfish bowl. Of the nine, eight should be colored and one black. Goldfish are excellent for improving the Feng Shui luck of a home or office and they work best when located in the north, the east, or the southeast of the home. They should never be in the bedroom.

Good Fortune

Good health, good family and prosperity luck. Good fortune luck includes all that one hopes for in life, specifically good health and longevity, wealth and prosperity, good family and descendants' luck, and a good personal reputation. Feng Shui promises all these if you live in harmony with your environment.

Good Luck

A specific type of luck in particular areas of your life. Luck is an abstract term and in Feng Shui it refers to the accomplishment or possession of specific categories of good fortune. Feng Shui lists eight types of good luck – wealth, health, family and relationships, children, having a good name, having a good career, having a good education, and having the goodwill of powerful people. Chinese divination readings define luck as different types and grades of luck for each of these eight categories. Money and **wealth luck** is subdivided into the luck of inheritance, the luck of gambling and speculation, and the luck of business success. In the language of Feng Shui luck thus has many different meanings.

Grass

On an empty patch of land, grass creates the auspicious **bright hall** when located directly in front of your home.

Grave Sites

These benefit enormously from the practice of Yin Feng Shui. The correct orientation of grave sites is part of Yin Feng Shui practice, a difficult and extremely potent branch of Feng Shui.

Green Dragon

The green dragon of Feng Shui is believed to be the earth dragon. There are nine dragons altogether – the others are wind, sea, water, sky, fire, golden, mountain, and celestial – each of which is reputedly the creature that controls one aspect of the universal **elements**. *See also* **Dragon**.

Greenhouses

Like gazebos, they can strengthen the Feng Shui of your door. Greenhouses represent additions to the home and these can be good or bad luck depending on the location of the main door. *See also* **Gazebos**.

Hanging Objects

Feng Shui cures represented by windchimes, bells, flutes, bamboo stems, etc. Such objects can be hung from beams and ceilings to counter inauspicious Feng Shui features. They should be unobtrusive and be hung as discreetly as possible.

Harmony

In Feng Shui this refers to the harmonious interaction of the **elements** in the living space. In Feng Shui everything in the universe can be categorized as being one of five **elements** – wood, fire, water, earth, or metal. For them to be in harmony, **elements** in each part of the living space should be mutually enhancing rather than mutually destructive.

Health Luck

This offers a vigorous, robust, and long life. Using specific parts of the Eight Mansions formula can activate good health luck. One auspicious personalized direction is the health direction. If you use **Tien Yi**, with your head pointing in the corresponding direction, this can enhance your health and physical well-being.

Heaven Luck

The luck with which you are born and over which you have no control. Heaven luck (or fate) exerts an influence over a person's life. You can improve your heaven luck by harnessing the powers of your earth luck. This is basically the practice of Feng Shui. Mankind luck is created by actions, choices, and behavior — whether or not one leads a virtuous life. Heaven, earth, and mankind luck are collectively referred to as the trinity of luck.

Hedges

Block out bad drain flows and negative sights. Growing a hedge to block out unsightly structures is very effective when these structures are facing you from the southwest and northeast. Hedges can be any height but they should not appear threatening by being too close to the home.

Hills

The natural undulation of the landscape where dragons live and a sure sign of potentially good Feng Shui. The **green dragon** lives in hills, creating auspicious breath and good energy. Hills should be rolling, with smooth gentle slopes, rather than sharp craggy cliff faces. Where vegetation is lush and green and there is a good balance of sunshine and shade, dragons and tigers are also said to be present. There are five types of hill shape, each one based on the five **elements** of fire, wood, earth, metal, and water. For Feng Shui analysis it is useful to develop the ability to discern these differences, which offer clues as to their suitability for each individual. Understanding the element connotation of hill shapes, or the shapes of their peaks, also enables practitioners to judge the Feng Shui quality of a range of hills.

Homes

The most important place for Feng Shui. Residential Feng Shui affects a person's overall luck. Even when Feng Shui at work may not be very good, if you have a house or a room with good Feng Shui your overall luck will be quite good. Residential Feng Shui is especially important for the well-being of families. In the home the three major features to get right from a Feng Shui perspective are the main door, the bedroom, and the kitchen.

Horse

The animal of the south, it can bring excessive **Yang energy**. The horse is a symbol of courage, speed, and perseverance and is also one of the treasures of Buddhism. It is auspicious to hang a painting or picture of horses in the south side of the living room because the element of the horse is fire, which coincides with the south direction. Horse figurines placed in the southwest are said to energize luck in social climbing and in the northwest for luck in examinations.

Horseshoe

In **Landscape Feng Shui** the ideal land formation. A house embraced by three ranges of hills forming a horseshoe and looking out onto flat land is said to have excellent Feng Shui for at least five generations.

Hostile Structures

These include buildings, land features, hills, outcrops, overhead roads, overpasses, and other large concrete structures that can send intimidating breath toward your home. *See also* **Poison Arrows**.

House

In Feng Shui anywhere that you eat, sleep, and take shelter is defined as your house. No matter how short your stay there, if the Feng Shui of the house is good it will benefit you. On the other hand, bad Feng Shui in such a temporary abode can also cause problems.

Rooms That Are Too Yin

Rooms that never see sunlight, are damp, decorated in only shades of gray and blue, narrow and cramped, always closed and silent, or which have been occupied for a long time by someone who has been chronically sick, have too much **Yin energy**. They cause sickness and bad luck to befall the residents. People who stay in rooms that have an excess of **Yin energy** suffer more than their fair share of misfortunes and seem to be shrouded by a cloak of bad luck.

Creating Yang energy

Try to create some **Yang energy** by doing the following:

- Repaint the walls with a bright Yang color – pinks, yellows, even red.
- Bring in the light. White walls are very Yang because they are bright.
- Throw away draping curtains and bring the sunlight into the room.
- Use happy colors for your curtains.
- Use bright colors for duvets, bed sheets and other soft furnishings.
- Keep the windows open.
- If trees are blocking the light from outside, cut them back.

- Install plenty of lights and keep at least one turned on continuously.
- Keep the radio or television turned on. Sound, light and laughter bring in **Yang energy**.
- Have vases of freshly cut flowers.
- Introduce movement with mobiles and windchimes. They symbolize life energy.

Rooms That Are Too Yang

If you play loud music all day long and your room is fitted with bright red furnishings and the walls are painted bright red or bright yellow, the energies are too Yang. There is too much noise and too much energy, so you would be well advised to introduce some Yin features to counter this imbalance. Observe some periods of silence during the day. Change your drapes to a darker Yin color or even install a blue light.

Similarly, if your home receives direct afternoon sun, the room is too Yang. Counter this by hanging some heavier drapes that cut out the glare of the sun. Or hang a faceted crystal that transforms the hostile sunlight into the bright colors of the rainbow, bringing in friendly **Yang energy** rather than killing **Yang energy**.

Observe that creating a balance of Yin and Yang in your home is an extremely subtle exercise.

Essentially, a room should have elements of Yin and Yang, but never too much of one or the other. Have music and life in the room, but not all the time. Have peace and quiet in the room, but not to the extent that it becomes lifeless. Have a cool décor of blues and grays, but also incorporate a splash of Yang color which may be represented by a vase of red roses or a painting of a sunrise.

Black and white color schemes are symbolic of Yin and Yang harmony, but there should also be sounds and life. A completely black and white décor that is always silent is regarded as much too Yin in the same way that if there is too much noise, it is regarded as too Yang.

Remember that Feng Shui is a subtle blend of opposite energies that complement each other. What you should always strive for is the harmony of opposites. This is the fundamental guiding principle of Yin and Yang.

Hsia Calendar

Also known as the Chinese **lunar calendar** and used in Feng Shui and fortune-telling. All fortune-telling and Feng Shui calculations using an individual's date of birth are based on the Hsia calendar. There are several methods in Feng Shui that require a person's birth details to discover their most auspicious sectors and directions. Fortune-telling methods include the Four Pillars of Destiny, which reveal character, personality, and future destiny. This method incorporates characters from the Chinese Hsia calendar extensively.

I Ching, or the *Book of Changes*

See **Book of Changes**.

Illness

This is often the first sign of bad Feng Shui. When occupants living in the same house take turns getting sick, or when children keep falling ill, these are indications that the Feng Shui of the home can be improved. Check to see if there are any **poison arrows** pointing directly at the home and therefore hurting it, then see if any of the drains around the house or building are blocked. Also make certain that your plumbing and your sewage system are in good order. Sometimes a simple course of action is enough to remove the obstacles that block the flow of **Chi** and cause bad luck.

Indoor Gardens

Placed in the correct sector of the home, these bring exceptionally good fortune. If you want an open-air design in your home that calls for indoor gardens and landscaped interiors, make sure that these are located in the east, the southeast, or the south sector of your home. Following this advice allows you to blend harmoniously with the elements that make up your living space.

Do not place your indoor garden in the sector that corresponds to the southwest or the northeast. This will cause disruptions in your family life and could also harm the marriage.

Interior Feng Shui

The arrangement of furniture to create auspicious vibrations. This refers to the layout of the home and the allocation of rooms according to Feng Shui guidelines. It also refers to the selection of curtains and carpets and other soft furnishings. The ideal Feng Shui home creates a warm ambience where **Yang energy** and auspicious **Chi** flow freely from room to room.

Jade Belt

This refers to any river and waterway that flows past your main door and seems to be "hugging" your home, bringing good fortune. If you also have hills behind your home this configuration is considered to be excellent Feng Shui. In such a case, enhance the good effect of the water by making certain it flows past your main door in the correct direction. Follow these guidelines:

- If the water is flowing from right to left (from inside the house looking out), your main door should face any of the four secondary directions, i.e. northeast, northwest, southwest, and southeast.
- If the water is flowing from left to right, your main door should be facing one of the cardinal directions, i.e. north, south, east, or west.

Jade Plant

An auspicious shrub that is regarded as the wealth plant. This refers to a variety of plant with succulent dark green leaves, which resemble a piece of precious jade. These plants are especially auspicious placed in the southeast corner or displayed in store windows where they will attract customers into the store.

Japanese Garden

More for meditation than for Feng Shui. The layout and design of Japanese gardens are based more on Zen principles that are excellent for meditation and contemplation than on attracting good fortune **Chi**. Japanese gardens, however, offer excellent creative ideas on the use of stones and pebbles and these can be incorporated into Feng Shui gardens that have a southwest or northeast facing aspect.

Jewelry

For personalized good fortune luck and protection. People wear jewelry today to attract luck-enhancing **Chi** and to generate protective physical energies in the same way as our ancestors used to wear amulets and charms. Jewelry adorned with auspicious symbols attracts good fortune. Thus, engagement and wedding rings with the double happiness symbol bring excellent marriage luck. Coin jewelry attracts wealth energy. Genuine jewelry is always better than fake – diamonds are more powerful than crystal, and gold or platinum are better wealth energizers than steel or fake gold.

Kan Trigram

Placed north, it signifies water and winter. The image is a single strong Yang line sandwiched between and being pressured by two Yin lines. Kan often signifies danger in that it warns that water is a double-edged sword that can go out of control, as when it breaks its banks and overflows. Kan also represents the north sector of any home.

Ken Trigram

Placed northeast and signifying the mountain or earth element. Its meaning represents keeping silent. It stands for patience and a time of preparation. To activate the **Chi** essence of Ken, place an object of the earth element (e.g. crystals, globe, sand, or boulders) in the northeast. This is particularly helpful for students.

Khen Hua

A rare white flower whose blooming signifies exceptional good fortune. This is a variety of succulent cactus, which flowers at midnight. The flower is large and white with yellow stamens. It is both fragrant and beautiful. The khen hua's very occasional flowering is believed to be a sign that descendants will have career and material success and will rise to prominence.

Killing Breath

Also known as **Shar Chi**, this brings grave misfortunes. It is the opposite of the good auspicious **Chi**. Killing breath creates havoc with your life and your luck and you should endeavor to dissolve, destroy, or deflect killing breath coming your way. *See also* **Poison Arrows**.

Kitchen

The part of the home with the potential to press down misfortunes. The placement and orientation of the kitchen is extremely important for the Feng Shui of any home. Kitchens (and especially the stove or oven) should never be located in the northwest of the home: this is described as a fire at heaven's gate. The kitchen is best located deep inside the home, closer to the back than the front; it is also better placed on the right of the front door rather than on the left side when you enter the home. If you practice **Compass Feng Shui** on **Kua numbers**, a practical use of the formula is to locate the kitchen in your worst (i.e. your Chueh Ming, or total loss) direction according to your **Kua number**. Do not site the kitchen in any one of your personalized auspicious sectors since this presses down on your good fortune.

Kua Numbers

Derived from the Eight Mansions formula for Feng Shui orientations. To determine your personal auspicious and inauspicious directions, first work out your personal Kua numbers. The calculation of this requires your year of birth and your sex. The year of birth must first be converted into the equivalent year according to the **lunar calendar**; do this by finding out whether you were born before or after the lunar New Year in your year of birth (*see* Chinese calendar, pp. 285–93). *See* "Compass Feng Shui," pp. 55–8, for advice on how to work out your Kua number.

Kun Trigram

The ultimate Yin **trigram**, denoting the place of the matriarch or the female maternal. Kun, meaning the receptive, is made up of three broken lines and represents the dark, the yielding, the primal power of Yin. Its image is big earth. It also symbolizes fertility. Placing this **trigram** in the children corner can help couples to conceive children. Being the ultimate Yin **trigram**, it can also be used to balance out excessive **Yang energy**; for example, if the afternoon sun is too strong for the house, displaying a Kun **trigram** might reduce the inauspicious effects of the sun. Kun is also an important symbol of the earth mother and activating the place of Kun, i.e. the southwest, brings good luck in areas associated with love, social life, family, and relationships with people in general.

Lake

An example of big water in front of the house, which brings good luck. The Feng Shui is considered to be very auspicious especially when the waters of the lake are clean, unpolluted, and teeming with life. In such conditions, the lake becomes a source of precious **Sheng Chi**. To harness fully the good luck of the lake apply the principles of the five **elements**. Thus, a lake to the north of your front door is better than a lake to the south. This can be engineered by the way you orient your home. Make certain that you have a view of the lake from inside your living room and under no circumstances position your home with the lake behind you.

Lamps

Used to simulate precious **Yang energy**, lamps are usually excellent Feng Shui when placed almost anywhere. Even in the north corner, which is the place of water, placing a lamp does not spoil the Feng Shui since **Yang energy** turns water into steam and this creates the symbol of power. Thus you can have lamps all over the home and they will bring good energy. Do not, however, have lamps too bright. Muted, warm lights are always better than harsh white lights. *See also* **Lights**.

Land Levels

The topography and contours of the land and their implications are an important part of Feng Shui investigation into particular sites. Land that is completely flat is generally regarded as inauspicious and can only be made habitable from a Feng Shui point of view if efforts are made to create variations in height and levels by introducing buildings to attract an auspicious flow of **Chi**. It is good Feng Shui to live with the mountain behind and therefore supporting one's home. The technique of Feng Shui is to orientate a home in such a way as to capture the maximum good **Chi** created by the presence of different land levels. *See also* **Landscape Feng Shui**.

Landscape Feng Shui

This is based on form, topography, and structure. Landscape Feng Shui is classical Feng Shui. Any practitioner must apply this method to an investigation of the site of any house before introducing other Feng Shui methods. Landscape Feng Shui is also known as **Form School** and, as the name suggests, it looks at the forms – the structures, shapes, topography, and levels of the land – to investigate the quality of the air and the **Chi**. The environment is believed to be alive with **Chi** and whether this is auspicious or not depends largely on the way the winds and waters have shaped the landscape over time. The practice of Feng Shui focuses on the best way to site and orientate the home in any given landscape such that superimposing the imaginary **four celestial creatures** becomes benign and auspicious rather than hostile or inauspicious.

Later Heaven Arrangement

The sequence of **trigrams** arranged around the **Pa Kua** and the one used in Feng Shui analysis for the abodes of the living. The Later Heaven arrangement is also known as the "inner world" arrangement where the **trigrams** are taken out of their groupings in pairs of opposites and instead are shown in a circular temporal progression of their manifestations within the physical earthly realm. What are perceived then are the cycles of the year with four distinct seasons, the cycles of each day with its day and night and so forth. Under this new arrangement, therefore, the cardinal points and the seasons are more closely related. This arrangement of the **trigrams** is thus drastically different from the **Early Heaven Arrangement**. *See also* "The Eight-sided Pa Kua Symbol," pp. 192–3.

Leaf Shapes

Analyzing the suitability of trees to particular sectors of the garden and the shape of their leaves can determine the luck of plants placed near the home. Thorny and prickly leaves should be discouraged. Round, succulent leaves are considered more auspicious than long knifelike leaves.

Lemon Tree

An indicator of good fortune when fully laden with fruit. Placed near the front of the house in the spring this indicates the ripening of good fortune. *See also* **Lime Tree**.

Li Trigram

Placed south it signifies fire. Li, meaning the clinging, is made up of one weak broken line in between two strong unbroken Yang lines. Li is fire, the sun, brightness, lightning, heat, and warmth. Since the south is the corner of the fire element, placing the Li **trigram** in the south is an effective way of activating the **fame luck** that the south sector can bring.

Lights

Excellent both for energizing good **Chi** and dissolving bad **Chi**. Lights are among the most versatile tools in Feng Shui practice. They correct numerous Feng Shui problems not only because they are a source of precious **Yang energy** but also because lights cause **Chi** energy to rise. They can solve problems of missing corners, excessively Yin corners, and land levels that are too low. Lights also attract good **Sheng Chi**, bringing customers to restaurants and good fortune to corporations that keep their front entrances well-lit. Placed in the south they are particularly auspicious and combined with crystals their potency is considerably enhanced.

Lilies

Yellow lilies represent vibrant **Yang energy** and are auspicious. It is far more auspicious to present a bouquet of yellow lilies than one of red thorny roses. White lilies are also a good fortune gift and are excellent for convalescing patients. They bring with them the pure and healing energy of the west.

Lime Tree

An auspicious tree to display during the lunar New Year. A lime tree heavy with ripening fruits symbolizes the ripening of good fortune and prosperity. These plants are usually seen at the entrances to the homes of Chinese families during the fifteen days of the lunar New Year. This symbolizes a prosperous start to the New Year. An orange plant will have the same effect. *See also* **Orange Tree**.

Lions

A pair of lions in front of the gate or main door is an excellent symbol of protection against bad **Chi** and against people with bad intentions trying to get into your home. The lions need not be enormous, and their size should be proportionate to the size of your door. Lions are an excellent alternative to **Fu dogs**.

Living Rooms

The best place in the house for locating Feng Shui enhancing and energizing symbols. The Feng Shui of living rooms and the way furniture is arranged in such rooms takes on significance in the overall Feng Shui of the home. The most auspicious part of the living room is the far end diagonal to its entrance. Placing something significant here, such as a favorite chair, will bring you to the luckiest corner. It is also a good place to display a three-legged frog and a dragon. Living rooms should always be on a lower level than bedrooms and dining rooms.

Lo Shu Magic Square

An important tool of analysis made up of nine sector grids. This square is probably the most important symbol in **Compass Feng Shui**. The Lo Shu grid was supposedly brought to the attention of the Duke of Chou on the back of a turtle that surfaced in the Lo River. The significance of the grid lies in its arrangement of numbers in a nine sector grid so that the sum of any three numbers in any direction adds up to fifteen, the number of days it takes for the new moon to become a full moon, and because of this co-relation the Lo Shu grid is said to offer clues to the fortunes of people and homes over a time period. Thus Lo Shu analysis very often centers on the time dimensions of Feng Shui. It is therefore the principal tool in the calculation of the **flying star** method of **Formula Feng Shui**.

Logos

Inauspicious logos can bring down a company. A corporate logo should always be designed with its Feng Shui significance in mind. Companies have benefited from auspicious logos, and some have gone under because of very inauspicious ones.

Longevity

An important Chinese aspiration similar to having good health, longevity is one of the most important components of having good luck. It implies the luck of seeing one's descendants succeed and bringing honor to the family name. It also means a life of good health. In symbolic Feng Shui the emblems of longevity are numerous, and the most important symbol is the **God of Longevity**, Sau Seng Kong. Other symbols are the pine tree, the bamboo, the peach, the deer, and the turtle. Displaying any of these symbols in the home is considered to bring excellent luck.

Lotus Pond

The lotus is a good fortune flower considered a symbol of enlightenment. A lotus pond is always an excellent feature in any garden, and is viewed as being extremely auspicious although not necessarily from a material point of view. Lotus ponds indicate a heightened sense of peace and mind transformation. They encourage spiritual development.

Lotus Seeds

Signify auspicious offspring luck. The seed of the lotus is an excellent symbol of descendants' luck. Displaying lotus seeds in the home is said to enhance and speed up the arrival of grandchildren. Buddhists value prayer beads made of lotus seeds.

Love

In the Chinese scheme of things this is used in reference to marriage and family luck. In the language of Feng Shui love is defined as the kind of luck that leads to marriage and for women especially a first marriage. For men, love is related to finding a woman who can take on the role of earth mother, who can bear children and keep house. This is not a very romantic view of love and it is certainly at odds with modern opinion and attitudes.

Lucky Numbers

Displaying lucky numbers prominently if the number of your house or building happens to be an auspicious one. Auspicious numbers are those that end in 1, 6, 7, 8, and 9, all of which are very lucky, although 8 is particularly popular among the Chinese because phonetically it sounds like "phat," which means "prosperous growth" in Chinese. Nine is considered by most Feng Shui masters to be the premier number because it signifies the fullness of heaven and earth. The numbers 1, 6, and 9 together in any permutation are considered the luckiest combinations. The number 8, which represents this period (the years 2003–2023), is considered lucky because it represents both current and future prosperity.

Most people cannot choose the numbers of their houses, their telephone numbers, or car license plates, but anyone who can should select a number with a lucky combination. An alternative is to play down any unlucky numbers by showing them small, but playing up a good number by showing it prominently. Some numbers are unlucky. The number 4 is considered the death number because phonetically it sounds like "sey," or "die," in Chinese. For many people, however, 4 has brought fabulously good luck! The combination of 2s and 3s together is considered extremely inauspicious: it leads to misunderstandings, quarrels, and other problems. The very worst number of all is 5. In Feng Shui this number brings nothing but problems and difficulties.

Lunar Calendar

The Chinese lunar calendar is divided into twelve months of twenty-nine days each. Every two and a half years an extra month is added to adjust the calendar and this extra month is consecutively interposed between the second and the eleventh months of the lunar year. An auspicious day of the lunar calendar is the "first day of spring," generally referred to as the "lap chun." Some years have double lap chuns (considered auspicious years) and some years have no lap chun at all (these years are considered bad luck for births and marriages). In the lunar calendar, the day begins at 11pm, and the twenty-four hours are divided into twelve segments of two hours each, with each one being ruled by one of the twelve animals. For divination purposes one must know the animal symbols that signify one's hour of birth and the animal that signifies one's year of birth. It is just as important to know the **elements** which rule one's four pillars and in the process understand the meanings of animals, **elements**, and the Yin–Yang connotations. The difference between good and bad luck lies in how these symbols are combined and Chinese fortune-telling involves interpreting these meanings.

Luo Pan

The Luo Pan, or authentic Chinese geomancer's compass, is an elaborately complex instrument comprising up to thirty-six concentric rings drawn around a small magnetic compass. *See* "The Luo Pan Compass", pp. 164–5.

The Luo Pan Compass

The Feng Shui compass is known as the Luo Pan. In the center is the actual compass which, like the western compass, has its needle pointed to the magnetic north. However, unlike Western convention, Chinese Feng Shui practitioners make their analysis using south as the benchmark.

Ancient texts on the subject place south at the top and Feng Shui symbols also correspond to south being at the top. In practice, however, the Chinese direction south is exactly the same as the south referred to by people in the West. Similarly, the Chinese direction north is exactly the same magnetic north used in the West. It is thus not necessary to use a Chinese Feng Shui Luo Pan. Any good western compass is perfectly adequate. Equally, it is not necessary to transpose the directions. Whether you live in the northern or southern hemisphere, and whether you live in the East or the West, all directions referred to are the actual real directions as indicated by an ordinary modern compass.

The Luo Pan is a reference tool used by Feng Shui masters, and veterans of the science usually have their own versions of the Luo Pan, containing summaries of their own notes and interpretations. These notes are jealously guarded as trade secrets and are placed in code in concentric rings around the compass. As the rings get larger, the meanings get deeper and refer to more advanced formulas. It is sufficient for the amateur practitioner to understand the first two inner rings of the compass and their meanings are illustrated here for easy reference.

When studying the Feng Shui compass, note that advanced Feng Shui uses secret formulas that examine the directions of doors, the flow of water, and the orientation of houses. These formulas divide each of the eight directions into three subdirections, thereby offering different recommendations for each of 24 possible directions. **Formula Feng Shui** requires very precise and careful measurements of compass directions.

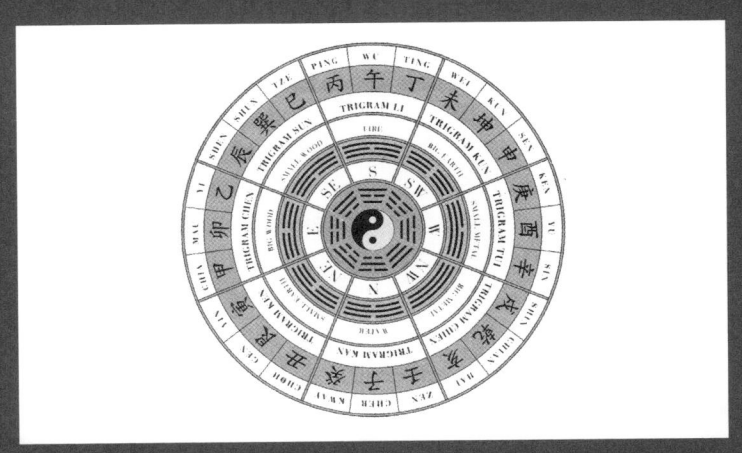

The first few rings of the Luo Pan show the relationship between the different symbols employed in Feng Shui practice.

Magnolia

An exquisite symbol of feminine sweetness and beauty. An especially good flowering shrub to grow in the west side of your home or in a west-oriented garden.

Mandarin Ducks

Wonderful symbols of conjugal happiness, which should be displayed. A pair of mandarin ducks is said to symbolize a young couple in love. According to symbolic Feng Shui displaying a pair of ducks in the southwest corner attracts the luck of romance and love. Ducks made of wood are not as effective as those made of jasper.

Mankind Luck

A part of the trinity of luck that you create for yourself. This is the kind of luck in the trinity of luck – tien, the luck from heaven; ti, the luck from the earth; ren, the luck people create for themselves. Of the three kinds of luck, both earth luck and mankind luck are within our control. Earth luck is Feng Shui and mankind luck is what we create for ourselves. *See also* **Tien Ti Ren**.

Marriage

Feng Shui is to do with activating the earth **elements** of the southwest. Just as bad Feng Shui cause havoc in the marriage, good Feng Shui can also create conjugal bliss and family harmony. To energize good fortune in marriage look after the place of the matriarch: this is the place of the **Kun trigram** – the southwest. The ruling element of this corner is big earth. Thus, objects that simulate or produce this element are said to be particularly good for activating marriage luck. Lights and crystals are thus excellent energizers.

Mattresses

One big mattress in the conjugal bed is much better than two separate single mattresses. These could cause a rift between husband and wife because they symbolically create a schism between the couple. It is better to have two completely separate beds, or even separate rooms, than to have one bed with two mattresses.

Mentor Luck

Such assistance from influential people is energized by activating the northwest. The northwest direction is important and takes on great significance because the **trigram** associated with it is **Chien**, which symbolizes the leader and blessings from heaven. Those in need of mentor luck and the support of powerful people should activate the flow of **Chi** in this part of the home. Hanging a six-rod windchime is one way of doing this because it creates the essence of metal energy.

Metal

One of the **elements** of Feng Shui represented in the west and northwest. Metal is also regarded as gold and the word in Chinese characters is the same. The metal element is made auspicious with the presence of earth since earth produces gold. Thus placing a symbolic earth element object such as a globe in the metal corners of your home brings success and wealth. Metal is destroyed by the fire element. This suggests that installing bright lights, for instance, in the metal corners would be disastrous for the luck of the corner. *See also* "The Five Elements," pp. 97–9.

Mirror

A major Feng Shui tool to use for business Feng Shui and other purposes. Mirrors are one of the prime Feng Shui tools and have many uses. They can be used to regularize the shape of a room. When there is a missing corner, for example, installing a wall mirror visually extends the wall outward, thereby filling up the missing corner and restoring the balance of the room.

Mirrors can also eliminate freestanding columns in the room. If you have a structural pillar in the middle of the room which you cannot knock down, wrapping it with mirrors in effect makes it "disappear." A column in the middle of the house is especially harmful, since it symbolizes a knife plunged into the heart of the home. If you do not wish to wrap the whole column with mirrors, use plants and creepers instead.

Placing a mirror in your dining room symbolizes the doubling of food on the table. Food has always been an important indicator to the Chinese of how well the family is doing, thus an abundance of food is always very good Feng Shui. Similarly, placing a mirror next to the cash register in a retail outlet will double turnover.

Mirrors can be used to reflect the **Shar Chi**, or **killing breath**, sent toward the front entrance of your home or office by **poison arrows**. Such **poison arrows** can also be countered using a **Pa Kua** or cannon, or by simply reorienting the front door. A mirror is a less hostile way of reacting to someone else's poison arrow hitting at you and should be used if it is enough to dissolve the **Shar Chi**.

Misfortunes

Those resulting from bad Feng Shui usually occur continuously. If you feel that a run of ill-luck is down to bad Feng Shui, check on the regularity of such occurrences. In practicing Feng Shui, be careful not to attribute all the bad or good things that happen to you solely to bad or good Feng Shui.

Money Luck

This is created with Symbolic and Water Feng Shui. There are specific measures recommended in Symbolic Feng Shui practice and in the practice of the Water Dragon Classic that are specifically focused on the creation of wealth and prosperity luck. Symbols of money are coins and the wealth deities and these can be displayed in the home to attract wealth-creating **Chi**. Energizing the southeast sector of the home with luscious plants or a water feature is also a popular method of activating money luck.

Money Plant

Creepers that symbolize the successful enhancement of income. The money plant is generally found in the tropics. It has yellow and green heart-shaped flowers. The money plant should not be confused with the jade plant. *See also* **Jade Plant**.

Moon Gate

A circular entrance is considered to represent an auspicious balance of Yin and Yang energies and was popular in old times. The round shape suggests the element of gold.

Mother Earth

The **Kun trigram** (made up of three broken lines) which rules the southwest symbolizes "mother earth" (i.e. big earth). It is the ultimate Yin **trigram** and signifies the female side of all of us. This **trigram** can be used to enhance relationship luck by doubling it, thus making it into the hexagram Kun (six broken lines), and hanging it in the southwest of the home or room. Another way to use mother earth to energize the southwest (the romance corner) is to display a large globe or map of the world as a representation of mother earth.

Mountain Star

A divinitive star used in **flying star Feng Shui** formulas. The mountain star is one of two divinitive "stars" used in this form of analysis. Mountain stars indicate good fortune for any sector they fly into when they carry the numbers 1, 6, or 8 and indicate extremely bad luck when the numbers are either 5 or 2. **Flying star Feng Shui** is probably one of the most advanced Feng Shui formulas and its interpretation and correct practice require many years of intensive study and experience. The other star used in this method of Feng Shui is the water star and analysis of the **flying star** chart usually requires that both the mountain and water stars are interpreted and analyzed together.

Mountains

Mountains in the environment are vital for good Feng Shui. Completely flat land, without undulation or elevated land forms, does not have the presence of the **green dragon** and is therefore inauspicious. You can symbolize the presence of a mountain in your home or office by hanging a picture of one; the mountain must always be behind you to symbolize solid support, to anchor you, and prevent you from being swept away by misfortune. In Feng Shui analysis, mountain shapes are categorized into five **elements** and orientations are classified as one of the **four celestial creatures**. In Feng Shui analysis today, large tall buildings (especially in cities) are considered in the same way as mountains were in ancient times.

Mou Tan Flower

See **Peony**.

Narcissus

See **Bulbs**.

Natal Charts

These offer a Feng Shui reading based on **flying star Feng Shui**. These are based on special calculations that indicate in some detail the luck of all the eight sectors of any house. The method used is **flying star Feng Shui**, which divides time into periods and calculates the natal charts of buildings based either on when they were first constructed or on the last time that they were extensively renovated.

Natural Contours

This refers to hills and mountains in the landscape, particularly those that simulate the dragon and tiger. **Landscape Feng Shui** looks at the natural land forms and elevations. However, man-made buildings also affect the Feng Shui of a site and are also taken into account.

Nien Yen

The personal direction to activate or energize for good family luck, love, and marriage. This is one of the four auspicious directions allocated to each **Kua number** in the Eight Mansions formula.

Noise

Noise is generally regarded as a manifestation of, and a way of simulating, intense, loud **Yang energy**. During the start of spring or at the start of the lunar New Year, people used to create noise by lighting firecrackers, which were believed to scare away any lingering evil spirits from the previous year. Sometimes hanging a fake firecracker in the house signifies the real thing and is supposed to simulate the creation of **Yang energy**. In Feng Shui, however, merely placing this symbol is deemed sufficient to simulate precious **Yang energy**.

North

Associated with the water element, it is also the place of the tortoise. The north part of your home should be energized with the presence of water. If you cannot place a real water feature, hanging a painting of a water scene is sufficient to keep the energies of the **elements** in harmony.

Northeast

The place of the earth element that also stands for education and scholarship. Displaying objects belonging to this element will keep the element energies in harmony.

Northwest

The place of the patriarch signified by the **Chien trigram**. This is probably the most important corner of any home because of its association with the patriarch, or family breadwinner. Always make certain that the energies of the northwest are kept alive and well. This is the place of big metals so placing earth or metal objects here is an excellent idea. Do not place fire in the form of lamps or lights in this area. Fire destroys metal in the cycle.

Numbers

The numbers 1 to 9 offer a multitude of good and bad Feng Shui. Numbers have connotations of good and bad luck according to Feng Shui. The general rule is to go with what the number sounds like. Thus, the phonetic sounds of each of the numbers 1 to 9 indicate that 3 and 8 are excellent numbers while the number 4 is to be avoided. Based on **flying star** analysis the numbers 5 and 2 are the villains while the numbers 1, 6, and 8 are supposed to be excellent. The number 9 is generally considered to be excellent.

Office Feng Shui

The same principles apply to Feng Shui at work as they do at home except that in the office the most important consideration is the energizing of wealth and harmony luck to ensure that employees work as comfortably as possible. The directions that benefit everyone will be in accordance with the birth date of the CEO or the most senior person in the office. To ensure the company is protected against downturns in business, the prosperity corner of the office should at all times be kept energized by the presence of a healthy fresh plant placed in the southeast.

Open Shelves

These resemble knives, which cut at you and cause untold harm. Their sharp edges send out **Shar Chi**, **killing breath**, and with it illness, loss of income, even a dramatic reduction in wealth. Try to block off any **poison arrows** being sent out by turning shelves into cupboards with the addition of doors. If you cannot do this, place books or files flush with the edges of the shelves to make them disappear. For shelves with ornaments, round off the sharp edges with sandpaper. Glass shelves are harmful in the north, wooden in the southwest, northeast, and in the middle of the room. Plastic shelves are the least harmful anywhere. *See also* **Bedrooms**.

Orange Tree

An orange tree is extremely auspicious and brings the family great **wealth luck**. This is because the Chinese word for orange, "kum," sounds phonetically like the word for gold. It is considered very lucky to display orange trees in fruit in the home during the lunar New Year, symbolizing a prosperous New Year to come. Because it is particularly good for energizing **wealth luck**, if you wish to plant an orange tree in the garden, it is best planted in the southeast corner (the wealth corner).

Orchid

An outstanding symbol of strength and bravery. In selecting plants for the garden, if the climate where you live is suitable, the growing of orchids signifies strength and courage as well as a lengthy stay in your career. Orchids are long-lasting flowers that bring good healthy **Chi** to the home.

Orientations

These refer to the directions of doors, and sitting and sleeping positions. Orientation is an important aspect of correct Feng Shui practice and it is often necessary to go to some length to take correct measurements and compass directions so that orientations are accurately implemented according to Feng Shui theory. Orientation can also mean the correct siting of the home to take advantage of auspicious features in the environment, such as rivers, lakes, hills, and fields.

Pa Kua

The eight-sided symbol used in the interpretation of good or bad Feng Shui. It corresponds to the four cardinal points of the compass and the four subdirections and derives its significance from the eight trigrams of the **I Ching**. *See* "The Eight-sided Pa Kua Symbol", pp. 192–3.

The Eight-sided Pa Kua Symbol

This is probably the most important symbol of Feng Shui. The eight sides represent many things in the practice of Feng Shui, and by itself, it is also believed to symbolize powerful protective energies. Chinese people around the world hang the Pa Kua above their main doors just outside their homes to guard against any killing energy that may inadvertently be shooting at them. This is usually caused by hostile objects or structures that represent **poison arrows**.

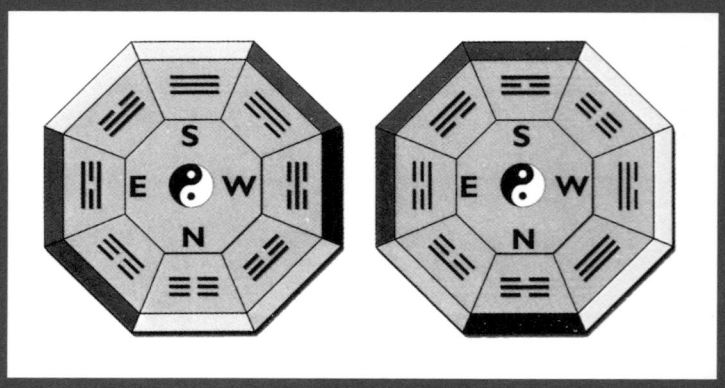

The Pa Kua of the Early Heaven Arrangement (left) and of the Later Heaven Arrangement (right).

In the vocabulary of Feng Shui, the Pa Kua used as a protective symbol is the Pa Kua of the **Early Heaven Arrangement**. This has the **trigrams** arranged around the eight sides in a different way from the Pa Kua of the **Later Heaven Arrangement**.

The Early Heaven Pa Kua is also used in the practice of Yin Feng Shui – the Feng Shui of grave sites for one's ancestors. The Chinese believe that the luck of descendants is hugely affected by the Feng Shui of their ancestors' graves.

For Yang Feng Shui – the Feng Shui of the dwellings of the living, which is what concerns most of us – the symbol of the Later Heaven Pa Kua is significant. Here the arrangement of the **trigrams** around the eight sides gives meaning to the eight major directions of the compass represented on the Pa Kua, with south always placed at the top. It allows for the correct interpretation and relationships of the other symbols of Feng Shui.

These other symbols are associated with numbers (one to nine), the five **elements** (water, fire, earth, wood and metal), the members of the family (father, mother, sons, and daughters), the **four celestial creatures** (turtle, dragon, tiger, and phoenix), and the characteristics of each of the **eight trigrams** themselves.

Pa Kua Mirror

The **Yin Pa Kua** used for deflecting **poison arrows**. It is usually painted with a red background to create masses of vital **Yang energy**, and the **trigrams** are placed round the **Pa Kua** in the Early or First Heaven arrangement. In the center is the mirror that reflects away all the hostile energy coming in its direction.

Park

A park or similar space located in front of your main door represents the auspicious **bright hall**. The effect is extremely good Feng Shui because **Chi** is said to be able to settle and accumulate before entering your home.

Pathways

Winding paths are better Feng Shui than straight pathways. Any path, driveway, and even corridor is less harmful if it is not straight and long. In the garden a winding pathway is best since it causes **Chi** to meander and this slows it down, allowing it to accumulate.

Patio

A patio is an excellent way of adding a missing corner. Depending on the direction in which the patio is located you can also enhance it with element therapy. Thus, for example, a patio located in the north will benefit enormously from a water feature, while a patio in the south could be made into a barbecue area.

Pavilions

Structures that can either strengthen or weaken the main door. *See also* **Gazebos**.

Paving Stones

A winding pathway of paving stones is an excellent feature in the earth corners of your garden.

Peach

The fruit of longevity. Displaying a peach branch in jade in the center of your home will attract longevity luck.

Peach Tree

Many legends surround the peach tree which offers immortality to anyone who eats its fruit. Supposedly growing in the western paradise, it is said to fruit once every 3,000 years.

Peacock

The peacock signifies dignity and beauty. For centuries, the attractive colors of the peacock's tail feathers have made them popular emblems of official rank, and fans made out of these feathers are often hung in Chinese homes. The peacock can also be used as a substitute for the **crimson phoenix**. *See also* **Phoenix**.

Peony

The king of flowers and excellent for creating good romance luck. The peony is associated with beautiful and desirable women. The legendary Yang Kuei Fei, reputedly one of the most beautiful women in Chinese history and concubine to the emperor, decorated her bedchamber with peonies all year round. The emperor, who could deny her nothing, had to arrange for these flowers to be sent to her from the south.

Parents who want their daughters to marry well should hang a large painting of many peonies in the living room. The more luscious the blooms, the better the fortune. Paintings of peonies, or peonies made of silk, can also be used in the bedroom, but activating the living area is better. If you are already married, hanging a picture of peonies in the bedroom will cause your husband to be more amorous, but perhaps with someone else. Peonies are therefore not good for bringing romance back into the marriage.

Pergolas

Garden structures that are an excellent solution for missing corners. These bring great variety to a large garden but do check carefully to see if they will add or detract from the Feng Shui of your home. *See also* **Gazebos**.

Period of Eight

The period of eight (2004–2023) belongs to the third son, the young man we nurtured who now understands the emotive side of his nature and is willing to show us the way. This age will be symbolized by the mountain (Ken). It will be a period when partnerships and ventures, which have stood the test of time, will come to an end or change, with the possibility of new directions surfacing, resulting in a challenge and a shift in policies. In the period of eight obviously the number 8 will be doubly lucky.

Phoenix

The bird of the south that brings great opportunities. Often depicted in Chinese mythology as the mate of the celestial dragon, the phoenix can be used as a Feng Shui symbol to activate the luck of opportunity. For marriage luck, the phoenix and the dragon together symbolize great conjugal happiness and the Chinese often use the dragon–phoenix symbol at wedding banquets. Place a dragon–phoenix motif in the southwest to activate marriage luck.

For **career luck**, a phoenix on its own symbolizes new opportunities. To activate luck in your job, a picture of the phoenix without the dragon is better because it releases the energy of the phoenix. With the dragon, the phoenix is a Yin creature; without the dragon it becomes a Yang creature, bringing financial success and prosperity.

In **Landscape Feng Shui**, the phoenix is represented by a small mound or slightly elevated land in the south, or at the front of the home. If you do not already have a small mound in front of your main door, you can artificially create one to energize the luck of the sector. As a creature of the south, the phoenix works best when placed in the south sector or corner of the home or office. If you cannot find a suitable phoenix symbol, other birds with fine plumage such as the rooster or peacock are also suitable.

Pillars

Pillars and columns have the potential to cause Feng Shui problems if they are freestanding and face a doorway directly. Square pillars cause more harm than round pillars. Two round pillars flanking a door is good Feng Shui. If pillars are causing problems because their edges are facing you, place a plant against the edge to "hide" the edge.

Pine Trees

The pine tree is a hardy symbol of longevity and strength in adversity. It is a good idea to have at least one pine tree in your garden. The leaves of the pine tree are also said to possess excellent qualities for cleansing the home of bad energies. They are thus useful media for space cleaning and purification.

Plants

Plants always signify good Feng Shui and are suitable enhancers of the wood corners of the home or office. Just as lights suggest the fire element, plants always suggest the growth essence of the wood element. If you grow plants around your home, and especially in the east and southeast, it will greatly enhance your Feng Shui. Keep plants under control by cutting them back and trimming them regularly. Dying plants should be discarded immediately.

Plum Blossom

Hang a picture of plum blossom to create a happy, long life. With the peony, the lotus and the chrysanthemum the plum makes up the four auspicious flowers. They also collectively represent the four seasons, with the plum signifying winter. The plum is commonly regarded as a symbol of a happy and long life because the flowers appear on the leafless and apparently lifeless branches of the tree until it reaches an extremely advanced age.

Poison Arrows

These are the harmful and hostile structures in the environment that send out killing energy toward your home. Learn to spot them and how to deflect them. Poison arrows have the power to destroy houses with even the best Feng Shui.

Looking out for poison arrows requires practice. Just remember that anything sharp, pointed, angular or hostile has the potential to harm you if it is directed towards your door.

- A common cause of **Shar Chi** is the triangular shape of the roof lines of a neighbor's house. If such a structure is facing you, try to reorient your door.
- Living near to or facing electrical transmitters or pylons often causes negative energies to build up. Shield them from view by growing a clump of trees between them and your home.

- A highway overpass that resembles blades hitting the front of your door also causes imbalance. Move away from such a house or building or hang a large windchime between the overpass and your front door.
- Directly facing a church, any kind of steeple, or a huge cross is inauspicious. Reflect back any negative vibrations with a **Pa Kua mirror**.

Other examples of structures that can emanate poisonous or **killing breath** at your home include signboards and pointers, windmills, sharp hills, tall buildings, cannons, and tree trunks. Remember that they are harmful from a Feng Shui point of view only if they are directly hitting, or facing, the front door. *See also* "How to Deflect Poison Arrows," pp. 206–7.

How to Deflect Poison Arrows

When dealing with poison arrows, try to match the element of the object used as a cure with the compass location where there is a problem. Listed here are six such objects that can be used to deal with poison arrows.

Windchimes

These are often excellent for countering the ill effects of protrusions from ceilings and structural beams. Metal windchimes are especially effective when they are hung in the west and northwest corners of rooms.

Plants

These are excellent for shielding and dissolving **Shar Chi**, especially when placed against corners. As they also symbolize growth, they are perfect Feng Shui when placed in the east corners of rooms.

Screens

These are extremely popular with the Chinese as they are good at blocking energy that is moving too fast. By slowing down the pernicious breath, screens transform harmful energy into auspicious energy.

Curtains

These are very effective when used to block out bad views of threatening structures that create **Shar Chi**. Use heavy drapes or chintz curtains. They are effective in any corner of the home, but select colors according to the **elements** of the corners. Use red for the south, dark blue for the north, green for the east, and white for the west.

Mirrors

These are powerful Feng Shui tools because their reflective quality has the effect of sending **Shar Chi** back to where it came from. Mirrors also widen narrow, cramped corners and extend walls to make up for missing corners. However, they should be used carefully. They must not reflect the main door, nor should they reflect toilets. Mirrors are auspicious in dining rooms but should not reflect the bed of the master bedroom.

Lights

These are powerful antidotes for all kinds of Feng Shui problems. They are especially good when used to dissolve the **Shar Chi** of sharp edges and protruding corners, particularly when placed in the south corners of rooms, except angular lights, which are not beneficial.

Pomegranate

This symbolizes the luck of many offspring, all behaving in a filial and respectful manner with a successful future ahead of them. The many seeds of the pomegranate make it a symbol of posterity. Many parents advise their young newly-wed second generation to display a painting or sculpture of a pomegranate in their bedroom to create the luck of having many healthy children.

Ponds

Water features that are best placed in the north, southeast, and east. Small ponds are extremely auspicious in these directions. Keep the pond well aerated with moving or flowing water. To bring good **Chi** into the home, keep fish or terrapins in the pond.

Prickly Plants

See **Cactus**.

Productive Cycle

The productive cycle of the five **elements** creates a harmonious blend of **Chi** in the living space and this creates good Feng Shui. This cycle indicates that wood produces fire, which produces earth, which produces metal, which produces water, which produces wood. Using this cycle to discover the suitability of one element to another, it is possible to arrange the objects in the living space to conform to the harmony of **elements**. *See also* **Wuxing**.

Protruding Corners

See **Columns and Pillars**.

Purple

An auspicious color, purple signifies water and is more special than blue. Purple is particularly lucky when combined with chrome and silver.

Quartz Crystal

Energizers for the southwest used to create romance luck. Natural crystal clusters are excellent emblems of the earth element and are therefore very suitable as energizers for the southwest and the northeast. These two corners are of interest to the younger generation since the southwest represents love and social life and the northeast signifies **education luck**.

Quiet Areas

The bedroom of the house should be a place of relative peace and quiet, where Yin **Chi** is to be preferred to too much Yang **Chi**. However, when the whole house is excessively quiet, luck remains stagnant.

Real Estate

A business signified by the earth element. Any kind of business involving property and property development will benefit from the energizing of the earth element in its business premises. Crystals, urns, terracotta pots and decorative stones can be used as good fortune symbols. Work them into the décor of the office or stores and make sure they are placed in the earth sectors, either southwest or northwest.

Rectangular Shapes

These represent the wood element and are most auspicious. The essence of the wood element is that it symbolizes growth. Thus rectangular shapes are also said to signify growth, also making the shape lucky.

Red

The most popular and auspicious color, red is the ultimate Yang color. It stands for the **Li trigram** and represents the fire element. Red strengthens and energizes wherever it appears, particularly in the winter when **Yang energy** is on the wane. Red is worn on all kinds of happy occasions. When you hang auspicious calligraphy in the home use red as the background color to make the calligraphy come alive. However, red can also cause serious problems when used in excess. If fire is not kept under control it can burn and destroy, therefore, control it and let it work for you.

Red Thread

Useful for tying onto auspicious symbols to energize **Yang energy**. Most symbolic objects of good fortune that are displayed benefit from the use of red thread. This signifies infusing the object with precious **Yang energy**, thereby making it come alive. Thus, when you place coins, boulders, three-legged toads, and other good fortune objects, tie a red thread around them to animate the Yang **Chi**.

Refrigerators

When placing a refrigerator in a kitchen, never put it next to the stove. This will create a clash of **elements** — water (representing the refrigerator, dishwasher, and sink) and fire (the stove). They should not be placed opposite each other either. Both such arrangements are bad Feng Shui.

Rice Urn

To the Chinese the rice urn symbolizes the rise and fall of family fortunes. Chinese who follow traditional practices take care to ensure that their rice urn is always well looked after. As the staple food to the Chinese, rice represents the family's livelihood. Wealthy Chinese matriarchs of the old school have been known to bequeath the precious family rice urn to the family of the eldest son. Some families in China continue to use urns that have been in the family for generations. A well-preserved rice urn passed from one generation to another will ensure that a family will remain wealthy even during difficult times. The family rice urn, like the symbolic **wealth vase**, should be kept tucked away in a storeroom, signifying the family's fortune being safely hidden away. Under the rice there is usually a carefully wrapped red packet containing gold coins to symbolize money. This money is renewed every lunar New Year to ensure continuous good fortune. Usually, if the last year has been a good one, one of the old coins will be kept and new ones added. This preserves the good luck the family has been enjoying for the year to come. The rice urn should be kept closed at all times. Use a strong urn to store your rice.

Rivers

A slow-moving river visible from your home is considered an auspicious Feng Shui feature. Rivers are believed to be purveyors of the good **Chi**, especially when the water is slow moving, meandering, and clean. Polluted rivers tend to be afflicted with poisonous breath. If your land is near a river orientate your house to face it. Then, depending on the direction the river flows past your front door, let your door face a direction that effectively captures the good **Chi** of the river. Do this by observing the guideline on water flow extracted from the Water Dragon Classic:

- If your door faces one of the cardinal directions – north, south, east, or west – the river should flow past the door from left to right. This direction is taken inside the house looking out as you face the river.
- If your door faces a secondary direction – southeast, southwest, northeast, or northwest – the river should flow past your door from right to left.

Roads

Surrounding roads have good or bad Feng Shui depending on their levels and directions. Roads that seem to hit directly at the home usually result in bad Feng Shui that should be countered with a **Pa Kua** or a mirror, or simply blocked off from view. Also, one should be wary of living near road junctions or intersections of any sort.

Rock

A rock or a boulder placed in a bathroom can overcome its bad effects. Rocks tied with red thread are an effective antidote for toilets that are located in the north part of the home. Toilets here cause bad luck for career professionals. Rocks can also be used to energize for good luck in the northeast and southwest of the garden. Here a small rock garden stimulates earth energy, which brings good family relationships as well as friendships.

Romance

This luck can be activated in the bedroom or the southwest corner. Feng Shui advises that by energizing the luck of the female maternal, i.e. the southwest corner, romance and marriage luck are stimulated. This can be done with a variety of symbols, which signify romance, love, and togetherness. A pair of mandarin ducks, the double happiness symbol, and crystal clusters are some of the objects that can be used for this purpose.

Rooftops

These should never have water features. If you have a rooftop garden and wish to energize the north corner with a small fish bowl, make sure it is not too large. You must not have a swimming pool on the rooftop, nor should you have a blue roof since symbolically water above a mountain spells danger.

Rooms

Different rooms located in different parts of the home can be allocated according to their orientations. One simple method of allocating rooms for family members is to try and place the patriarch's bedroom in the northwest, and the matriarch's bedroom in the southwest. Young sons should be placed in the east and young daughters in the west. Use the **Pa Kua** arrangement of **trigrams** to guide you in the allocation of rooms for the children. *See also* "Feng Shui Tips for Interiors," pp. 224–5.

Round

Because the circular shape denotes the metal element it can also stand for gold. Round shapes are especially suitable in the west, northwest, and north and they can be incorporated into structures and designs used in these corners of the house or garden.

Feng Shui Tips for Interiors

Good Feng Shui starts with the main door, which should open outward to an empty space, termed the **bright hall**, where the cosmic **Chi** can settle and accumulate before entering your home. It should also lead into a space that is not too cramped. This allows **Chi** to gather before meandering through your home.

- The main door should never open into a cramped hall. Install a bright light if the space is too narrow.
- The main door should never open directly into a staircase. Place a screen in between or curve the bottom of the stairs.
- There should not be a toilet too near the main door. This causes **Chi** that enters the home to become sour.

Well-lit and clean apartments attract auspicious energies. Small, dark and unused corners create **killing breath**, so air store rooms occasionally. Do not have too many doors opening from a long corridor; this will cause quarrels. The ratio of windows to doors should not exceed 3:1. Doors should not directly face a window, as **Chi** will come in and go out again.

- Three doors in a straight line are deadly Feng Shui. The **Chi** is moving too fast. Hang a windchime or place a dividing screen in front of the middle door.
- Toilets and bathrooms should not be located in the north corner of the home, as this flushes away career and promotion opportunities for the breadwinner.
- Staircases should ideally be curved and winding. Spiral staircases resemble a corkscrew and are harmless when placed in a corner, but deadly when located in the middle of the home.
- Rooms should be regular in shape, with kitchens located in the back half of the home.
- Dining areas should be higher than living rooms if there are split levels.

The ideal arrangement of rooms will encourage **Chi** to move smoothly through your home.

Sailing Ship

Filled with false gold, a model sailing ship is one of the more effective Feng Shui energizers and symbols to have in the home. This is especially effective for bringing good business luck.

Sculptures

Effective Feng Shui enhancers which bring good fortune when placed in the earth corners of the garden. Sculptures made of stone, granite, marble, or in ceramic form are suitable for the southwest and northeast. Metallic sculptures suit the west and northwest. Avoid sculptures with sharp points or angles.

Seasons

Each season has a corresponding element. Winter is of the water element; wood is spring; fire is summer; metal is autumn. Earth is the element for the period in between seasons.

Shade

As important as sunlight, shade adds to the balance of Yin and Yang and is necessary in any environment, a garden or otherwise. However, too much shade in place of sunlight makes for excessive **Yin energy**.

Shar Chi

Killing energy, or **killing breath**, caused by **poison arrows** and an imbalance between Yin and Yang. Shar Chi is the antithesis of **Sheng Chi** and Feng Shui prescribes various cures to counter it.

Sharp Edges

The sharp edges of corners or buildings create some of the most serious forms of **Shar Chi.** If the entrance to your house or property is being hit by the sharp edge of a building across the road, try to block it from view. Alternatively, use a **Yin Pa kua mirror** to ward off killing energy. *See also* **Pa Kua Mirror.**

Sheng Chi

The dragon's cosmic breath which brings energy and growth. If you tap Sheng Chi you are sure to enjoy good health, prosperity, and peace.

Silver

A very auspicious color when combined with purple. In Chinese the word for silver is "ngan." When combined with purple – "chee" – it becomes "ngan chee," which literally means money. In Feng Shui silver belongs to the metal element and is symbolic of the west and northwest.

Sleeping Positions

Compass Feng Shui gives each person a **Kua number**, which then determines an individual's four best and four worst sleeping directions. It is advisable to sleep with your head pointing toward one of your good directions.

Slopes and Contours

These have significant Feng Shui connotations. It is always preferable to live on the middle level of a slope than at the top or the bottom, embraced by contours on three sides with the back of the house supported by the slope. At the top of the slope the house is exposed to the elements; at the bottom auspicious **Chi** will "sink."

Small Water

In Feng Shui this generally refers to artificially created water features, such as water in domestic drains and the way it flows, which are not part of the natural landscape.

Social Life

Promote your social life by using bright lights to give a boost to the **Yang energy** in the southwest corner of your garden. This is the place of big earth and it creates great amounts of energy. If you do not have a southwest part of the garden, or if you live in an apartment without a garden, you can install a similarly effective light if you at least have a balcony or terrace in the southwest. Use two lights rather than one: two is the number of the southwest.

For those living in small apartments without a terrace, the living room can be energized in the same way by placing a bright lamp in the southwest corner. A red lamp will strengthen the symbolism of **Yang energy**. The lamp used should be neither too large nor too small and it should be at least 5 feet (1.5m) from the ground, as a standard lamp, a table lamp, or hanging from the ceiling. Note that this does not apply to the bedroom.

South

The place of the phoenix, the summer season. South represents fame and is generally considered one of the happiest directions of the compass. According to the Yang Dwelling Classic, if you site your house with a south-facing orientation it will bring you extremely good Feng Shui. In the south part of your living room keep the corner well lit. Placing something red in this corner is also excellent. *See also* **Phoenix**.

Southeast

This is the corner to energize if you want to increase your income. Use plants and water to attract income to this corner. Identify the location of this corner with a compass.

Southern Hemisphere

North is always north. Countries in the southern hemisphere should definitely not change the compass directions when applying and using **Compass Feng Shui**.

In recent years some Western writers have attempted to apply Western scientific rationales to Feng Shui to make a case for the compass directions to be flipped when applying Feng Shui in countries south of the equator, such as Australia. They contend that this is due to winds from the north being "hot" in the southern hemisphere, since the equator lies to the north. From this they conclude that the element for the compass direction north should be fire, not water. Similarly they contend that the element for the south is water not fire. This single change has repercussions on the interpretation of Feng Shui all the way through the formulas and this also affects systems of Chinese astrology and fortune-telling.

Authentic Chinese Feng Shui masters reject this line of interpretation. They point to the placement of the **trigrams** around the **Pa Kua** as being the arbiter of the element assigned to each of the compass directions. Thus, in the north the **trigram** placed there according to the **Later Heaven** sequence is **Kan**, which stands for water, and hence the north is traditionally associated with water. In the south the **trigram** is **Li**, which is symbolic of fire. Thus the element here is said to be fire. The representations of the **trigrams** give each of the compass directions their different meanings and have nothing to do with the so-called "north winds" blowing into Beijing. This is speculation as to the origins of generalized Feng Shui guidelines based on recommendations given in the Yang Dwelling Classic, which advises that the front of the house faces south and the back faces north.

Latter-day practitioners, in speculating on the basis for this recommendation, have tried to explain it in terms of wind temperatures. It is important that the compass directions are not turned, making north south and vice versa. This is an absurd interpretation that can give rise to horrific mistakes.

Southwest

The corner of ultimate Yin and good **Yin energy**, the southwest is a very important direction that benefits the family matriarch. If she is a central force in the home, make sure this direction is not afflicted by the presence of a toilet or a kitchen. An afflicted southwest corner also hurts the marriage prospects of the children.

Spring

The season of the wood element and the time of the year that represents growth and new beginnings; from a Feng Shui perspective it is also a good time to start a new business, launch a new product, or simply start a project or venture in business. The exact date of launching anything, however, should also be done with reference to the Tong Shu. *See also* **Almanac**.

Statues

Statues of the patriarch should be placed in the northwest while statues of any other members of the family should be aligned according to their auspicious directions. Statues also create excellent Feng Shui if placed in the southwest or northeast.

Steps

Connecting levels of the garden should conform to landscape guidelines, which state that levels being joined by steps must be correct. The levels of the back of the house should be higher than the front and land on the left-hand side must be higher than land on the right-hand side. If your house is located above road level and steps lead up to your front gate this is regarded by some as a most auspicious feature.

Stove

See **Cooking**.

Streams

Slow moving fresh water represents excellent Feng Shui. If you have such a feature in front of you, try to orientate your home so that the front door is facing the stream and also make sure the flow of the water is correct. Try not to waste this most auspicious Feng Shui.

Study

If you work from home pay special attention to getting the Feng Shui of your office correct since this will affect your livelihood and your professional reputation. Energize your office with all the relevant good fortune symbols but continue to observe all the taboos and recommendations for office Feng Shui.

Succulents

Any kind of succulent plant or fruit is deemed to be auspicious since it suggests that there is sufficient water to keep it alive and healthy. Succulent cactuses without thorns are excellent in place of jade.

Sun Trigram

This **trigram** is formed by two Yang lines above a single broken Yin line. Known as "the gentle", it is placed southeast on the **Pa Kua**. It represents the eldest daughter and its element is wood.

Sunlight

Sunlight brings pure **Yang energy** into your home. Wherever possible, windows and doors should be oriented to catch sunlight.

Swimming Pools

Must be placed strategically otherwise they cause problems. It is very easy to go very wrong with pools. The guideline is to place them on the left-hand side of the entrance door (inside looking out), otherwise the marriage could end in separation or even divorce. Ideally pools should not be square or rectangular in shape. Instead they should have rounded edges that do not hurt the home. Pools should never overwhelm the house. They should not be so large as to create an imbalance.

Remember that too much water is a sign of danger because when water overflows its banks it causes excessively bad luck. It is the same with the presence of natural water. When the body of water is large, it is good to be located a little away from it, so that the **Chi** wafting toward your home is both balanced and auspicious.

Symbols

Feng Shui is full of different symbols that spell good fortune. Learning to place them correctly and in the correct sectors of the home is part of Symbolic Feng Shui.

Tai Chi

A form of exercise based on the energizing of **Chi** flows inside the body. The movements are slow but very precise. Though it originated in China, Tai Chi has attracted and benefited millions of practitioners worldwide.

Ten Emperor Coins

A symbol that represents the wealth of ten reign periods. A very popular feature to hang in the office, placed strategically either behind your chair or on your left side to simulate the dragon, is coins taken from each of the ten emperors' reign periods tied together with red thread. The coins used can either be genuine antique coins from ten different reign periods or copies. In Feng Shui it does not really matter if you use fake coins or real coins, but some people believe that genuine antique coins carry the **Chi** of their period or origin.

Terrapins

Placed in the north, these domesticated turtles bring good fortune. It is excellent Feng Shui to keep one or six terrapins in the north sector of the home, be it in the garden or in a courtyard inside the home. If you are able, build a small waterfall which falls into a circular pond with a maximum size of about 3 feet (1m) in diameter. Keep terrapins in this pond, feeding them special food or fresh green leafy vegetables. The terrapins will grow rather large. Keep them as part of your household for they soon learn to recognize you. They bring great **Chi** to your home, ensuring a long life for the patriarch, and excellent children who bring honor to the family. They also bring wealth, prosperity, and protection for the home.

   If you are unable to find terrapins, you can have tortoises instead. They are land creatures and should not be kept in the pond. And if you are unable to build a pond, keeping a ceramic tortoise can symbolize the same kind of energies and is believed to be just as effective, especially if the imagery is accurate.

Thorns

Flowers and plants with thorns (such as roses and some cactuses) do not bring good Feng Shui and in fact cause slivers of **poison arrows** to attack you. Do not place such plants too near you where you work. Over time they will cause problems and difficulties to build up.

Three Feeling Water

The orientation of water that is good for your house. The Water Dragon Classic describes three good feeling water orientations that spell prosperity and success. There are also the seven sentiment waters, which spell bad luck and misfortune. Generally speaking, water is said to be excellent if it comes toward you in a wide form and leaves you in a narrow form, or when it has two or three small branches flowing into the main river that then passes your home. A third auspicious flow of water is when it seems to embrace your home like a jade belt. Water should never seem to flow away from your home in full view of the front door. This always means wealth flowing out. *See also* **Jade Belt**.

Tien Ti Ren

Heaven, earth, and mankind, the three types of luck referred to as the trinity of luck. This establishes the perspective of Feng Shui luck which is the luck of the earth. One is born with **heaven luck** but mankind luck is self-created. These three types of luck account in equal measure for the kind of success and happiness we experience in life. Earth luck and mankind luck are within our control while **heaven luck** is beyond our control.

Many Feng Shui masters believe that, when you have excellent **heaven luck** and lead a virtuous life, you automatically have good Feng Shui without your even being aware of it. You will get your orientations correct and you will display all the correct symbols of good fortune.

Tien Yi

The personalized direction to create good health, also called "doctor from heaven" direction. This is generally regarded as the direction that taps good health. It is a personalized direction that is based on the Eight Mansions Kua formula.

Tiger Hills

The range of hills that lie to the right of your house. According to **Form School** Feng Shui, land on the right-hand side of your home (the direction taken from inside the home looking out) represents the dragon hills irrespective of the actual compass direction. According to **Compass Feng Shui**, however, the west side of your home represents the tiger hills. The author usually uses the **Form School** method in her own Feng Shui.

Time Dimension

Time is an important consideration in Feng Shui philosophy and the cycles of time determine a building's prosperity and well-being. With the interplay between people and their environment, the prosperity of a building, whether it is a business or a home address, will ultimately affect the residents of that structure and the activities within it. Based on Feng Shui principles, time is divided into cycles of 180 years. These cycles have three sixty-year periods each, called upper, middle, and lower. Three ages of twenty years duration are contained in each period, resulting in a total of nine ages for each 180-year cycle.

Toilets

Toilets are always considered to be harmful Feng Shui. Do not decorate the bathroom with expensive fittings, flowers, and fancy adornments. Making it prettier does not enhance it from a Feng Shui point of view. It merely magnifies the bad luck. Bathrooms should be as small as possible, with minimal decoration. The bathroom door should always be kept closed and auspicious objects kept away from it. For example, hanging peonies for love in your romance corner, which happens also to house your toilet, may make you find love, but love that could cause you a lot of heartache.

Tortoises

Like turtles, tortoises are considered by the Chinese to be extremely auspicious. They attract good fortune into the household and protect you from bad luck. Like the turtle, they are associated with the north sector and the number one. If you decide to keep a tortoise in your home, it is better to keep a single tortoise. Since they require minimal care, they are easy to keep. If you are unable to keep a real tortoise, a figurine of a tortoise in the north corner will effectively symbolize the tortoise energy.

Traffic Flow

In cities, roads are now interpreted in the same way as rivers used to be.

Thus traffic flows are considered to be similar to river flows. Fast-moving traffic creates **Shar Chi** while slow-moving traffic creates **Sheng Chi** and is far more auspicious. Traffic lights and traffic calmers near your office or home are thus excellent since they force the traffic to slow down. However, traffic jams are bad Feng Shui since they signify a blocking of the flow.

Trees

These generally represent excellent Feng Shui but it is important that they be trimmed and kept in shape. Broad-leafed trees are effective cures for severe Feng Shui problems. They not only block incoming **poison arrows** but they also form an effective visual wall which can also double up as back support for any house lacking this vital **"black turtle"** support. Trees that possess good green foliage are excellent Feng Shui energizers for the east and the southeast corners. Trim them regularly in order that fresh shoots are always discernible. These signify continuous growth and the **Chi** generated is most auspicious. Avoid palm trees since their long trunks can cause Feng Shui problems. Trees standing in groups do not cause problems but single trees are similar to freestanding columns and emit harmful killing energy.

Triangle

This indicates the fire element and is an aggressive symbol that can harm a home when any of its three points are aimed at the entrance of the home. The triangle is often regarded as a protective symbol and is considered excellent when placed in the south because it is the symbol of fire.

Trigrams

Made up of three lines each, the trigrams are the root source of the hexagrams of the **I Ching** (the **Book of Changes**) upon which most Chinese divinatory sciences are based. Each trigram has its own special meaning. The predictive power of the **I Ching** is harnessed through the formation of hexagrams, which are usually created or built by tossing three Chinese coins. Each hexagram is made up of two trigrams. As well as making divinations trigram symbols can also be used as Feng Shui enhancers in the home.

Tui Trigram

The **trigram** that spells joyousness. It also describes the young woman who brings happiness. The west is considered the place of the young daughter because this **trigram** also indicates a lake. If there is a lake to the west of your home it spells the Feng Shui of happiness for your house.

Umbrella

A symbol of shelter that the Chinese believe should never be opened inside the house. The modern umbrella, as opposed to the old-fashioned parasol, is an acceptable variation on the symbol.

Unicorn

The Chinese unicorn, also known as the dragon horse, is considered a creature of good omen. It symbolizes longevity, joy, grandeur, illustrious offspring, and wisdom. The unicorn is said to possess qualities of gentleness, goodwill, and benevolence towards all other living creatures. It is an animal of solace and appears only when a particularly benevolent leader sits on the throne, or when a notable sage is born.

Urns

Symbolic receptacles with Feng Shui significance. Placed strategically, urns can bring wonderful good fortune in that they can signify the advent of great wealth. Wealthy Chinese often place a pair of big urns on either side of their entrance door inside the house. The urns have long necks and are kept empty symbolically to signify a vacuum waiting to be filled with wealth. Others prefer the broader based variety which they fill either with rice grains or "pretend gold." Urns filled with semi-precious stones are transformed into wealth urns that symbolize and attract wealth. Urns can be placed either side of your house to absorb noise and to neutralize anything causing you distress.

Vases

Can be transformed into wealth receptacles to attract good fortune. *See also* **Wealth Vase**.

Verandas

All verandas in the house are considered to be part of the home for the purposes of undertaking Feng Shui analysis. Since no one actually lives or works in these parts of the home, it can be said that the auspicious parts of the veranda are entirely wasted. They are good places, however, to hang windchimes. The enchanting sounds of windchimes in the northwest and west bring excellent **Chi** into the home.

Walls

The walls of your home can be painted in colors that enhance the element of their location or you can hang paintings and display auspicious objects to energize specific types of good fortune. *See also* **Color** and **Art**.

Water

This signifies wealth and correct water brings enormous prosperity. Water plays a very big part in Feng Shui recommendations. Although water is also an element of potential danger according to the **I Ching**, and should thus be treated with respect, it is also the element with the greatest potential for making you rich. For the years up to 2043 water is auspicious when placed in the north, the east, the southeast, and also in the southwest. The north and east are the best locations for water features either in your garden or inside your home.

Water Dragon

This represents the water formula's best configuration of water flow. There are specific instructions on how to build a Water Dragon in the Water Dragon Classic. This is part of the **Compass Feng Shui** formula on water flows and water exit directions.

Water Lilies

An excellent substitute for the lotus, the auspicious water lily symbolizes purity. If the fish in your pond or similar water feature are being pestered by birds, planting water lilies will give them protection.

Waterfalls

If you have the land and the budget to do it, building a small waterfall on the north corner of your land is excellent. Make sure that the waterfall is proportional to the size of your house and that the water does not appear to be flowing away from you. Keep the water trapped in front of a window or a door. This symbolizes the luck coming into your home and bringing good fortune. Also make sure the sound of water is soft, rhythmic, and friendly rather than loud. If you are using a pump, opt for the less powerful pump. Remember that slow-moving water is better than fast-moving water.

Wavy Lines

A wavy line incorporated into the design motif makes it a water element design suitable for the north, the east, or the southeast of your home or room.

Wealth Luck

One of eight major types of luck that Feng Shui can generate. Prosperity luck is one of the more obvious and welcome manifestations of correct Feng Shui practice. Simple wealth-enhancing techniques use Symbolic Feng Shui. Thus you can energize for wealth by displaying the three-legged toad or sticking Chinese coins in appropriate places to attract money **Chi**. It is also possible to energize the southeast with plants or to build a water feature in the north. Probably the most enduring Feng Shui wealth feature is a **Water Dragon**. Build one if you can.

Wealth Vase

A personal wealth vase is an excellent way to attract wealth Feng Shui. Your wealth vase can be made of earth or metal **elements**. Earth element vases could be porcelain or crystal, while metal element vases are made of copper, brass, silver, or gold. The more precious the material the vase is made of, the more auspicious it will be. The vase can be filled with semiprecious stones such as crystal, malachite, amethyst, citrine, and so on. You can also put your jewelry in the vase. Your wealth vase should be kept hidden away, inside a cupboard in your bedroom, and never facing your front door; this represents your wealth draining away.

Wells

A well is a useful feature to design into the water flow of your house. One of the most important parts of good water flow is to control the exit direction of all the waters of your home. You can do this effectively and efficiently by building a "well," which collects all the water of the home and then allows it to exit in the direction deemed most auspicious for you, based on the Water Dragon Classic formula.

West

If you want to create good descendants' luck in your home to benefit the children (the next generation), energize the metal **Chi** of the west part of your home. Do this by using white colors, displaying metallic items, and objects such as bells and singing bowls. One of the most effective ways of harnessing the metallic energy of the west is to use an authentic singing bowl to create the clear sound that attracts auspicious **Chi**. Strike the bowl three times with a special wooden mallet.

Western Sunlight

Usually excessively Yang. You should reduce the intensity of the afternoon sun by hanging small faceted crystals that can break up the sunlight into a rainbow of lights. This not only softens the severity of intense **Yang energy** but also reestablishes the cosmic balance. Creating rainbows inside the home will create happiness for the family.

White Tiger

A celestial creature of the west that complements the **green dragon**. The white tiger is basically a creature that protects the abode. Without the tiger the dragon is said not to be a genuine dragon. The tiger is the wrathful side of Feng Shui. Always keep the tiger under control by ensuring the west does not dominate. For instance, do not allow the west side, or tiger side, of any home to be higher or larger than the east side. Let the dragon remain supreme by using bright lights to keep the tiger under control. Avoid hanging pictures of tigers in your home: few homes can cope with the energy given off by such images.

Windchimes

Windchimes are among the most delightful and easiest methods of creating a good feeling in any home. Their tinkling attracts excellent **Sheng Chi**. Do not hang metal windchimes in the east or southeast: these are wood corners. Instead hang bamboo windchimes in these corners. Metal windchimes should be hung in the west and northwest while ceramic windchimes can be hung in the southwest and northeast. Windchimes energize and correct bad vibes. If you use a windchime to suppress bad luck or to deflect killing energy caused by a poison arrow, hang a hollow five-rod metallic windchime. If possible acquire windchimes that have the design of a pagoda: this is the symbol for trapping killing energy and malignant spirits.

Wind

Much of landscape is said to be carved by wind. Avoid places that are excessively windy, such as the top of a mountain or a seashore. When winds become too ferocious, they turn malevolent and carry killing **Chi**. Protect your home against harsh winds, whether they are warm or cold.

Windows

Homes without windows lack openings for the good Feng Shui to flow in, but there should not be too many windows in any home. The ideal ratio of windows to doors is 3:1. Windows that open outward are better than sash windows, but do not worry if you have the latter. Windows should not be placed on walls that are directly facing the entrance door. They are best placed on walls that are on either side of the entrance door. Again, this is the ideal situation and you do not need to worry too much if your windows go against this guideline. Windows that are directly opposite the entrance allow **Chi** to fly out the window. Under such circumstances, you will find it difficult to save money.

Wood

One of the five **elements** but the only one with intrinsic life energy. Thus the wood element signifies growth and is an excellent element to have in all the corners of the home. Life energy signifies **Yang energy**, which makes for auspicious Feng Shui. The directions that correspond to the wood element are east and southeast and the **trigrams** are **Chen** and **Sun** respectively. *See also* "The Five Elements," pp. 97–9.

Wuxing

The Chinese name for the five **elements**: "Wu" means "five" and "xing" is the shortened form of "five types of **Chi** dominating at different times." This has been shortened to "elements." Water dominates in winter, wood in spring, fire in summer, and metal in fall. At the intersection between two seasons, the transitional period is dominated by earth. Water, wood, fire, metal, and earth refer to substances whose properties resemble the respective **Chi** and help us understand the different properties of the five types of **Chi**. The properties of the five types of **Chi** are summarized as follows:

- *Water* runs downward; there is always danger of overflow.
- *Wood* grows upward; an excellent representation of life and growth.
- *Fire* spreads in all directions; radiant, hot, and able to get out of control.
- *Metal* pierces inward; sharp, pointing, and can be deadly and powerful.
- *Earth* attracts and nourishes; stable, caring, and protective.

See also "The Five Elements," pp. 97–9.

Yang Dwelling Classic

One of the older texts and classics, said to contain a comprehensive treatise on the practice of **Landscape Feng Shui**.

Yang Energy

Intrinsic nature of life energy, brightness, daylight, the sun. This is basically the life half of the Yin–Yang concept. Yang energy is symbolized by activity, by bright light, and by daytime hours. Yang energy is vital for the presence of good Feng Shui in the houses of the living, but it should never be present in such excessive quantities that Yin becomes obliterated completely. When Yin is completely absent, Yang ceases to exist.

Yang Pa Kua

The **Pa Kua** is used for analyzing and providing guidelines on how the corners of the compass can be energized to enhance their qualities. The whole of Feng Shui practice takes its cue from this arrangement of the **Pa Kua**. Those who advise that the directions of the compass be changed for southern hemisphere countries are attempting to rewrite the **Pa Kua**'s sequence of **trigrams**. It will render all their Feng Shui recommendations wrong and even create harmful results.

Yap Cheng Hai

The author's Feng Shui mentor. Yap Cheng Hai comes from an impressive Feng Shui lineage. A Chinese Classics scholar well versed in Chinese heritage and traditions, his expertise spans six decades. He has learned from many other masters (now deceased) and schools of Feng Shui in Hong Kong, Taiwan, and Singapore. He has ventured into Yin Feng Shui, visiting countless Chinese cemeteries to study ancestral burial sites. The Chinese believe that the orientation of ancestral graves also has an influence on the fortunes of their descendants. The study of authentic Yin Feng Shui is considerably more complex and difficult than Yang Feng Shui. Master Yap is particularly skilled in the practice and interpretations of Parc Chai (Eight Mansions school), San Yuan (**flying star** school) and, most renowned of all, the Water Dragon Classic (Water Feng Shui). Water Feng Shui's main promise is the serious enhancement of wealth. Master Yap's work and his success in this area of specialization have gained him an international reputation.

Yearly Reference Tables

Calculated to identify good and bad days. *See also* **Almanac**.

Yin Energy

Death energy, silence, darkness, the moon. **Yin energy** is the diametrical opposite of **Yang energy** but they do not conflict; rather they complement each other. In other words one follows the other and one gives life to the other. Yin energies are more suitable for houses of death, grave sites, burial grounds, and cemeteries. Yin is darkness and total silence but is also excellent energy for places of rest like the bedroom.

Yin Pa Kua

The **Pa Kua** that Feng Shui masters believe possesses "heavenly attributes" and thus is said to invoke the powers of heaven to dissolve, deflect, and fight back against hostile **killing breath**. This arrangement is reproduced on **Pa Kua mirrors** that are hung up outside above doors to fight against T-junctions or intersections and triangular roof lines, among other **poison arrows**. The Yin **Pa Kua** should never be hung inside the house.

Yin–Yang Symbol

This eloquently describes the balance of the two opposing yet complementary energies. It shows the ebb and flow of the energy and also signifies that in Yin and Yang there is always a little of the other present. Yin always gives rise to Yang and vice versa and when they are in complete balance the whole of Tao is said to be achieved.

Yellow

Yellow is considered to be as auspicious and as Yang as red. Because yellow used to be the Imperial color and ordinary citizens were not allowed to use it in their clothes or at home, red became the popular favorite and a symbol of good fortune. However, where no such taboo exists you might want to energize the auspiciousness of yellow. Thus bouquets of yellow flowers are said to be very lucky, as are yellow packets of money and yellow curtains and interior décor.

Appendix

The Chinese Calendar

An important aspect of Feng Shui practice uses a person's date of birth and ruling year elements to determine the suitability of directions for doors and orientation for sleeping and working. Use the calendar here to convert Western birth dates into the equivalent Chinese dates for later analysis of Kua numbers. Take note of your birth year element, as this lets you know which elements will be auspicious for you.

Year	From	To	Element
1900	31 Jan 1900	18 Feb 1901	Metal
1901	19 Feb 1901	7 Feb 1902	Metal
1902	8 Feb 1902	28 Jan 1903	Water
1903	29 Jan 1903	15 Jan 1904	Water
1904	16 Jan 1904	3 Feb 1905	Wood
1905	4 Feb 1905	24 Jan 1906	Wood

Year	From	To	Element
1906	25 Jan 1906	12 Feb 1907	Fire
1907	13 Feb 1907	1 Feb 1908	Fire
1908	2 Feb 1908	21 Jan 1909	Earth
1909	22 Jan 1909	9 Feb 1910	Earth
1910	10 Feb 1910	29 Jan 1911	Metal
1911	30 Jan 1911	17 Feb 2012	Metal
1912	18 Feb 1912	5 Feb 1913	Water
1913	6 Feb 1913	25 Jan 1914	Water
1914	26 Jan 1914	13 Feb 1915	Wood
1915	14 Feb 1915	2 Feb 1916	Wood
1916	3 Feb 1916	22 Jan 1917	Fire
1917	23 Jan 1917	10 Feb 1918	Fire
1918	11 Feb 1918	31 Jan 1919	Earth
1919	1 Feb 1919	19 Feb 1920	Earth

Year	From	To	Element
1920	20 Feb 1920	7 Feb 1921	Metal
1921	8 Feb 1921	27 Jan 1922	Metal
1922	28 Jan 1922	15 Feb 1923	Water
1923	16 Feb 1923	4 Feb 1924	Water
1924	5 Feb 1924	24 Jan 1925	Wood
1925	25 Jan 1925	12 Feb 1926	Wood
1926	13 Feb 1926	1 Feb 1927	Fire
1927	2 Feb 1927	22 Jan 1928	Fire
1928	23 Jan 1928	9 Feb 1929	Earth
1929	10 Feb 1929	29 Jan 1930	Earth
1930	30 Jan 1930	16 Feb 1931	Metal
1931	17 Feb 1931	5 Feb 1932	Metal
1932	6 Feb 1932	25 Jan 1933	Water
1933	26 Jan 1933	13 Feb 1934	Water

Year	From	To	Element
1934	14 Feb 1934	3 Feb 1935	Wood
1935	4 Feb 1935	23 Jan 1936	Wood
1936	24 Jan 1936	10 Feb 1937	Fire
1937	11 Feb 1937	30 Jan 1938	Fire
1938	31 Jan 1938	18 Feb 1939	Earth
1939	19 Feb 1939	7 Feb 1940	Earth
1940	8 Feb 1940	26 Jan 1941	Metal
1941	27 Jan 1941	14 Feb 1942	Metal
1942	15 Feb 1942	4 Feb 1943	Water
1943	5 Feb 1943	24 Jan 1944	Water
1944	25 Jan 1944	12 Feb 1945	Wood
1945	13 Feb 1945	1 Feb 1946	Wood
1946	2 Feb 1946	21 Jan 1947	Fire
1947	22 Jan 1947	9 Feb 1948	Fire

Year	From	To	Element
1948	10 Feb 1948	28 Jan 1949	Earth
1949	29 Jan 1949	16 Feb 1950	Earth
1950	17 Feb 1950	5 Feb 1951	Metal
1951	6 Feb 1951	26 Jan 1952	Metal
1952	27 Jan 1952	13 Feb 1953	Water
1953	14 Feb 1953	2 Feb 1954	Water
1954	3 Feb 1954	23 Jan 1955	Wood
1955	24 Jan 1955	11 Feb 1956	Wood
1956	12 Feb 1956	30 Jan 1957	Fire
1957	31 Jan 1957	17 Feb 1958	Fire
1958	18 Feb 1958	7 Feb 1959	Earth
1959	8 Feb 1959	27 Jan 1960	Earth
1960	28 Jan 1960	14 Feb 1961	Metal
1961	15 Feb 1961	4 Feb 1962	Metal

Year	From	To	Element
1962	5 Feb 1962	24 Jan 1963	Water
1963	25 Jan 1963	12 Feb 1964	Water
1964	13 Feb 1964	1 Feb 1965	Wood
1965	2 Feb 1965	20 Jan 1966	Wood
1966	21 Jan 1966	8 Feb 1967	Fire
1967	9 Feb 1967	29 Jan 1968	Fire
1968	30 Jan 1968	16 Feb 1969	Earth
1969	17 Feb 1969	5 Feb 1970	Earth
1970	6 Feb 1970	26 Jan 1971	Metal
1971	27 Jan 1971	15 Feb 1972	Metal
1972	16 Feb 1972	2 Feb 1973	Water
1973	3 Feb 1973	22 Jan 1974	Water
1974	23 Jan 1974	10 Feb 1975	Wood
1975	11 Feb 1975	30 Jan 1976	Wood

Year	From	To	Element
1976	31 Jan 1976	17 Feb 1977	Fire
1977	18 Feb 1977	6 Feb 1978	Fire
1978	7 Feb 1978	27 Jan 1979	Earth
1979	28 Jan 1979	15 Feb 1980	Earth
1980	16 Feb 1980	4 Feb 1981	Metal
1981	5 Feb 1981	24 Jan 1982	Metal
1982	25 Jan 1982	12 Feb 1983	Water
1983	13 Feb 1983	1 Feb 1984	Water
1984	2 Feb 1984	19 Feb 1985	Wood
1985	20 Feb 1985	8 Feb 1986	Wood
1986	9 Feb 1986	28 Jan 1987	Fire
1987	29 Jan 1987	16 Feb 1988	Fire
1988	17 Feb 1988	5 Feb 1989	Earth
1989	6 Feb 1989	26 Jan 1990	Earth

Year	From	To	Element
1990	27 Jan 1990	14 Feb 1991	Metal
1991	15 Feb 1991	3 Feb 1992	Metal
1992	4 Feb 1992	22 Jan 1993	Water
1993	23 Jan 1993	9 Feb 1994	Water
1994	10 Feb 1994	30 Jan 1995	Wood
1995	31 Jan 1995	18 Feb 1996	Wood
1996	19 Feb 1996	7 Feb 1997	Fire
1997	8 Feb 1997	27 Jan 1998	Fire
1998	28 Jan 1998	15 Feb 1999	Earth
1999	16 Feb 1999	4 Feb 2000	Earth
2000	5 Feb 2000	23 Jan 2001	Metal
2001	24 Jan 2001	11 Feb 2002	Metal
2002	12 Feb 2002	31 Jan 2003	Water
2003	1 Feb 2003	21 Jan 2004	Water

Year	From	To	Element
2004	22 Jan 2004	8 Feb 2005	Wood
2005	9 Feb 2005	28 Jan 2006	Wood
2006	29 Jan 2006	17 Feb 2007	Fire
2007	18 Feb 2007	6 Feb 2008	Fire
2008	7 Feb 2008	25 Jan 2009	Earth
2009	26 Jan 2009	13 Feb 2010	Earth
2010	14 Feb 2010	2 Feb 2011	Metal